COMPACT *Research*

# Marijuana

## by Andrea C. Nakaya

Drugs

ReferencePoint
Press™

San Diego, CA

**For more information, contact**
ReferencePoint Press, Inc.
17150 Via del Campo Road, Suite 204
San Diego, CA 92127
www.ReferencePointPress.com

Picture Credits:
AP/WideWorld Photos, 9, 15
Tamia Dowlatabadi, 33–35, 48–51, 64–68, 81–84

Series design and book layout:
Tamia Dowlatabadi

LIBRARY OF CONGRESS CATALOGING-IN-PUBLICATION DATA

Nakaya, Andrea C., 1976–
  Compact research : marijuana / by Andrea C. Nakaya.
    p. cm.
  Includes bibliographical references and index.
  ISBN-13: 978-1-60152-000-5 (hardback)
  ISBN-10: 1-60152-000-X (hardback)
  1. Marijuana—Juvenile literature. 2. Marijuana abuse—Juvenile
literature. I. Title.
  RC568.C2N34 2007
  362.29′5—dc22
                                                    2006030852

# Contents

# Foreword

**"Where is the knowledge we have lost in information?"**

—"The Rock," T.S. Eliot

As modern civilization continues to evolve, its ability to create, store, distribute, and access information expands exponentially. The explosion of information from all media continues to increase at a phenomenal rate. By 2020, some experts predict the worldwide information base will double every seventy-three days. While access to diverse sources of information and perspectives is paramount to any democratic society, information alone cannot help people gain knowledge and understanding. Information must be organized and presented clearly and succinctly in order to be understood. The challenge in the digital age becomes not the creation of information, but how best to sort, organize, enhance, and present information.

ReferencePoint Press developed the Compact Research series with this challenge of the information age in mind. More than any other subject area today, researching current events can yield vast, diverse, and unqualified information that can be intimidating and overwhelming for even the most advanced and motivated researcher. The Compact Research series offers a compact, relevant, intelligent, and conveniently organized collection of information covering a variety of current and controversial topics ranging from illegal immigration to marijuana.

The series focuses on three types of information: objective single-author narratives, opinion-based primary source quotations, and facts and statistics. The clearly written objective narratives provide context and reliable background information. Primary source quotes are carefully selected and cited, exposing the reader to differing points of view. And facts and statistics sections aid the reader in evaluating perspectives. Presenting these key types of information creates a richer, more balanced learning experience.

For better understanding and convenience, the series enhances information by organizing it into narrower topics and adding design features that make it easy for a reader to identify desired content. For example, in *Compact Research: Illegal Immigration*, a chapter covering the economic impact of illegal immigration has an objective narrative explaining the various ways the economy is impacted, a balanced section of fifteen primary source quotes on the topic, followed by facts and full-color illustrations to encourage evaluation of contrasting perspectives.

The ancient Roman philosopher Lucius Annaeus Seneca wrote, "It is quality rather than quantity that matters." More than just a collection of content, the Compact Research series is simply committed to creating, finding, organizing, and presenting the most relevant and appropriate amount of information on a current topic in a user-friendly style that invites, intrigues, and fosters understanding.

# Marijuana at a Glance

## Marijuana Use

Marijuana is the most commonly used illicit drug in the United States. Approximately 96.8 million Americans ages twelve and older have tried marijuana at least once during their lifetimes.

## Medical Marijuana

Americans disagree on the medical benefits of marijuana, even at high levels of government. Although marijuana is illegal under federal law in the United States, twelve states have legalized medical marijuana.

## International Marijuana Laws

Many European countries see no benefit to making marijuana illegal. Marijuana has been decriminalized in Great Britain, the Netherlands, Belgium, Germany, Croatia, Switzerland, Italy, Spain, and Portugal, among others.

## Enforcement

While U.S. marijuana use has stayed at about the same levels in recent years, arrests have increased dramatically, rising 113 percent between 1990 and 2002.

## Marijuana Abuse

Marijuana abuse is common; of the estimated 6.9 million Americans who abuse or are dependent on illicit drugs, 4.2 million abuse or are dependent on marijuana.

## Marijuana Treatment

Treatment and prevention of marijuana abuse costs billions of dollars every year; in 2003 it cost the federal government $3.3 billion.

## Health Effects

Critics disagree on whether or not marijuana is dangerous. In 2004 marijuana use was a factor in 215,665 emergency room visits in the United States; however, no one has ever died from a marijuana overdose.

## Pain Relief

Medical marijuana advocates claim that marijuana relieves pain and discomfort associated with cancer, AIDS, glaucoma, Alzheimer's disease, and multiple sclerosis. Opponents say relief is available through other means.

## Legalization

Support for marijuana legalization has increased in recent years. According to a 2005 Gallup poll, approximately one-third of Americans believe marijuana should be legal, up from only 12 percent in 1969.

# Overview

Overview

> **❝ Cannabis [marijuana] continues to be, by far, the most widely used drug in the world. ❞**
>
> —United Nations Office on Drugs and Crime, 2006 World Drug Report

**M**arijuana is the most commonly used illicit drug in the United States. According to a 2004 survey by the Office of National Drug Control Policy (ONDCP), approximately 40.2 percent of Americans ages twelve and older have tried this drug at least once during their lifetimes. Marijuana is also an illicit drug in most other nations, yet as in the United States, it is commonly used elsewhere. This widespread usage occurs despite continuous disagreement over its health effects and social impact, and amid intense debate over whether or not it should be legalized for medical or recreational use.

## How Marijuana Works

Marijuana is a mixture of flowers, stems, seeds, and leaves of the hemp plant *Cannabis Sativa*. It contains hundreds of chemical compounds, but the main active ingredient is THC (delta-9-tetrahydrocannabinol). The flowers of the hemp plant contain the most THC; the leaves contain less, and the stalk contains the least. Over time, marijuana growers have used crossbreeding to develop plants with higher THC levels, and to influence other characteristics such as taste or plant yield.

While this drug can be mixed with food or drink, it is most commonly smoked. When a person smokes marijuana, inhaled THC passes

*Marijuana, or Cannabis, contains many chemical compounds. The main active ingredient is TCH, the chemical that makes users experience a "high."*

from the lungs into the bloodstream and is carried to different parts of the body. When it reaches the brain and other organs, THC connects to specific sites on nerve cells, called cannabinoid receptors, and influences the actions of those cells. This leads to effects such as the "high" that users experience. Cannabinoid receptors are found in parts of the brain that influence pleasure, memory, concentration, sensory and time perception, movement, and coordination.

## Historical Use

Written texts from China and India indicate that marijuana was utilized there as a medicine more than two thousand years ago. Evidence also shows that it was used many years ago in Africa, the Middle East, Southeast Asia, South America, and Europe. Common uses included treatment for malaria, constipation, and rheumatism; as a headache remedy; for appetite stimulation; and as a sleep aid.

Marijuana was also legal and widely used in the United States for many decades. Beginning in the 1840s, American physicians began to prescribe it for a variety of ailments, including pain, depression, and insanity. It was widely available for purchase in drugstores. According to medical anthropologist Merrill Singer, marijuana was the most commonly prescribed pain medication in the United States until 1901 and it was available in high doses. "The daily dosage levels of cannabis that were prescribed for adults, pregnant women, and children are similar to what contemporary illicit users might consume in a month."[1] Beginning in 1901, however, as the effectiveness of aspirin was recognized and other synthetic drugs were developed, the popularity of prescription marijuana began to diminish.

## Restricting Marijuana Use

By the 1920s, not only was marijuana less popular, but many people began to view it as a dangerous substance. This belief was fueled by exaggerated stories of its harmful effects, circulated by the media and worried citizens. For example, a 1927 *New York Times* article claimed that a woman and her children went insane eating marijuana leaves. "The mother will be insane for the rest of her life," the reporter writes, and "there is no hope of saving the children's lives."[2] Official reports intensified public anxiety: For instance, one federal campaign launched during this period alleged a connection between marijuana and violent crimes and mental deterioration. In response to widespread concern over marijuana use, the federal government passed the Marijuana Tax Act of 1937. The act did not prohibit the drug, but it had the effect of a ban by making it expensive and difficult to obtain. Growers, sellers, and buyers were subject to taxes and strict registration and reporting requirements.

> **Marijuana was the most commonly prescribed pain medication in the United States until 1901.**

## Marijuana Prohibition

With the rise of experimental drug use in the counterculture movements of the 1960s, marijuana consumption increased again as many Americans, especially young adults, began to use the drug recreationally. Concerned about this and the use of other drugs, in 1970 Congress passed the Controlled Substances Act, aimed at regulating the manufacture, distribution, and possession of certain drugs. The act created five categories, or schedules, of drugs based on criteria such as a drug's potential for abuse and addiction and its accepted medical uses. Marijuana was included in the most dangerous and highly controlled category, called Schedule I, drugs that the government has determined to have a high potential for abuse and no currently accepted medical use.

The act has been amended several times since 1970, but numerous attempts to change the scheduling of marijuana have all been unsuccessful. For example, in 1972 President Richard Nixon established the National Commission on Marijuana and Drug Abuse, but ignored the panel's suggestion to decriminalize marijuana for personal use. A number of bills to allow the medical use of marijuana have also been introduced in Congress, but none have passed. Thus, marijuana remains illegal under federal law. Some states have passed their own laws allowing for the medical use of marijuana. However, under the Controlled Substances Act, federal agents have the right to investigate, arrest, and prosecute medical marijuana patients, caregivers, and providers.

> **The [U.S.] government has determined [marijuana] to have a high potential for abuse and no currently accepted medical use.**

While marijuana is also an illicit drug in most other parts of the world, a number of countries have decriminalized it, meaning that users might be subject to confiscation or a fine, but not imprisonment. In most countries, though, marijuana traffickers are still subject to harsh penalties. Countries that have decriminalized possession of small amounts of marijuana for personal use include Spain, Italy, Portugal, Belgium, Germany, Croatia, Switzerland, and Great Britain. Canada and the Netherlands have some of the most liberal marijuana policies in the world. In Canada, with a doctor's recommendation marijuana can be used for medical purposes. The Netherlands permits the possession and sale of small amounts of marijuana for personal use, and it is sold in licensed coffee shops there.

## Health Effects

Despite the fact that marijuana is illegal in most countries, there is widespread debate over whether or not it is actually harmful to health. People on both sides of this debate draw on a large body of research on the subject, both scientific and anecdotal, to support their position. Critics of marijuana use, for example, point to U.S. National Institute on Drug Abuse (NIDA) warnings that marijuana increases the risk of a heart attack, in smoked form is harmful to the lungs and respiratory system, and also impairs memory, learning, and social behavior. Many marijuana users counter such claims with personal testimony, insisting that they have never experienced any harm from marijuana use and have enjoyed many benefits of the drug. For example, writing under the pseudonym "Emancipated," one twenty-six-year-old marijuana user likens it to a "daily vitamin."[3] Another argument in favor of decriminalization is that marijuana is no worse than other legal and commonly used drugs such as alcohol and tobacco. Director of the Drug Policy Alliance Ethan A. Nadelmann asserts that marijuana use is similar to alcohol or pharmaceutical drugs that help people fall asleep at night or cope with depression or anxiety.

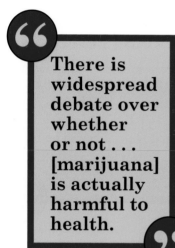

There is widespread debate over whether or not . . . [marijuana] is actually harmful to health.

## Extent of Use in the United States

Even though marijuana is illegal and its safety questioned, it is widely used in the United States. In 2004 the ONDCP found that 96.8 million Americans ages twelve and older have tried marijuana at least once during their lifetime. Approximately 3.2 million persons reported using marijuana on a daily or almost daily basis. Research shows that overall, adult use of marijuana has stayed at about the same levels in the past decade. However, some subgroups of the population show changes in usage. A 2004 study in the *Journal of the American Medical Association* (*JAMA*) found that among African Americans and Hispanics, marijuana abuse or dependence has risen over the past ten years. Among youth, marijuana use has declined in some age groups. According to the December 2004 annual federally funded Monitoring the Future survey, conducted by the University of Michigan, marijuana use by eighth-, tenth-, and twelfth-graders has been in a slow decline since 1996. However, the National Center on Addiction and Substance Abuse (CASA) at Columbia University points out that despite this decline, marijuana is still widely used by teens, with almost half of all high school seniors having tried it at least once.

## Prevention and Treatment

The U.S. government spends billions of dollars trying to prevent marijuana use and treating people who do use the drug. According to NIDA, of the estimated 6.9 million Americans who abuse or are dependent on illicit drugs, 4.2 million abuse or are dependent on marijuana. In 2003 government treatment and prevention programs cost $3.3 billion, up from about $2.2 billion in 1993.

> In 2003 government treatment and prevention programs cost $3.3 billion.

Most marijuana abuse begins at an early age, finds NIDA. According to its most recent data, 56 percent of marijuana abusers began to abuse marijuana by age fourteen, and 92 percent were abusers by age eighteen. Preventing abuse is difficult in part because, according to most youth, marijuana is easy to obtain. The Substance Abuse and Mental Health Services Administration (SAMHSA) confirmed in 2004 that many youth do not have to make any effort to get illegal drugs such as marijuana; rather, sellers offer buyers steady supplies. SAMHSA found that more than half of youth age twelve to seventeen believed marijuana was easy to obtain.

## Liberalization in the Netherlands

When discussing the effect of marijuana on society, some people look to the Netherlands, a nation that has relaxed its enforcement of marijuana laws. Researchers Alain Joffe and W. Samuel Yancy reviewed studies on marijuana usage in the period from 1984 to 1996, when there was virtually no criminal prosecution of marijuana-related offenses in the Netherlands. They found that overall marijuana use in the Netherlands increased as a result of this policy. Data show a steep increase until 1992, when the rate of increases began to slow. The increases from beginning to end, however, are still substantial. For example, the percentage of eighteen- to twenty-year-olds who reported ever having used marijuana increased from 15 percent to 44 percent.

The impact of such increases is less clear. The federal Drug Enforcement Administration (DEA) maintains that liberalization has increased drug abuse and crime in the Netherlands. It has also negatively affected society, says the DEA, with habitual use leading to a generation of young people who are passive and disinterested in personal achievement. Researcher Patrick Marshall contends that despite increasing use, the Dutch do not appear to believe that marijuana is harming their society. Not only have there been no calls for tighter marijuana regulation there, says Marshall, but there is pressure for even greater liberalization of marijuana laws.

## Marijuana as Medicine

While some people use marijuana as a recreational drug, others believe it has therapeutic value and should be legalized for medicinal use. Medical marijuana advocates claim it reduces the dementia of Alzheimer's patients, stimulates the appetite in cancer and AIDS patients, lowers high eye pressure caused by glaucoma, relieves muscle stiffness and spasms caused by multiple sclerosis, controls nausea in cancer patients undergoing chemotherapy, reduces the nausea and vomiting that AIDS and AIDS medications can cause, prevents seizures in some epileptic patients, and relieves chronic pain.

**The federal government insists that there is no evidence that marijuana should be accepted as medicine.**

Many sick people believe that marijuana is far more effective than any legal, prescription medication. For example, Californian Angel Raich uses marijuana to relieve the chronic pain and the symptoms of an inoperable brain tumor. She unsuccessfully sued the federal government in 2005 to continue her use of medical marijuana under state law. According to Raich in a legal declaration, "My life was saved by [marijuana]. . . . I can not stop using medical cannabis or I will die. I am not giving up the miracle I have been given to save my very life."[4] However, most government agencies do not agree with arguments such as Raich's. In the United States, the federal government insists that there is no evidence that marijuana should be accepted as medicine. According to Andrea Barthwell, former deputy director at the ONDCP, "Marijuana, whatever its value, is intoxicating, and it's not surprising that sincere people will report relief of their symptoms when they smoke it. The important point is that there is a difference between feeling better and actually getting better."[5]

## Medical Marijuana in Canada

In 2001 Canada became the first country in the world to legalize medical marijuana at the national level. Under its *Marihuana Medical Access Regulations,* people who are suffering from grave and debilitating illnesses are allowed to use marijuana if they obtain a doctor's approval. A 2001 study by the Medical Marijuana Information Resource Centre reported that an estimated 2 percent of Canadian adults might be using marijuana for medical purposes.

As in the Netherlands, the relaxation of marijuana laws in Canada coincides with increased general marijuana use. In 2004 the Canadian

*Many believe medical Marijuana should be legal so those who are ill can use it to ease their symptoms. This woman, who injured her back, has a prescription for medical marijuana.*

Addiction Survey found that 44.5 percent of Canadians reported using cannabis at least once, up from 23.3 percent in 1989. However, there are some negative reports associated with this increase. The study found that one in twenty people reported a marijuana-related concern, most commonly the failure to control their own use or concern about a friend's use.

## Medical Marijuana in the United States

Under the 1978 Investigational New Drug (IND) Compassionate Access Program, medical marijuana is legally available to some people in the United States. This program, established by the U.S. Food and Drug Administration (FDA), allowed patients with serious medical conditions whose symptoms could only be relieved with marijuana to apply for and receive medical marijuana from the federal government. Less than one hundred people were admitted to the IND program over the next fourteen years. Then in 1992 the program was shut down in response to the large numbers of AIDS patients making applications. Currently seven people still continue to receive marijuana through the program.

> " Twelve states have legalized medical marijuana use. "

For anyone else, medical marijuana is currently illegal under federal law. However, many states have passed their own laws to protect medical marijuana users. These various laws allow patients to grow, possess, and use medical marijuana, and physicians to discuss it with patients or recommend it to them. Twelve states have legalized medical marijuana use: Alaska, California, Colorado, Hawaii, Maine, Maryland, Montana, Nevada, Oregon, Rhode Island, Vermont, and Washington. Numerous other states have passed favorable medical marijuana laws, but this legislation is mostly symbolic since it does not override federal law or provide effective legal protection for medical marijuana users.

## Federal Marijuana Policies

Marijuana advocates have been extremely critical of federal policies on medical marijuana. Many believe that the continuing ban on medical marijuana is based more on politics than on reality. They charge that the government is steadfastly opposed to marijuana use, even therapeutic use, and refuses to hear any evidence undermining that position. According to doctor Kate Scannell, "The federal obsession that keeps marijuana out of the hands of sick and dying people is appalling and irrational. Washington bureaucrats—far removed from the troubled bedsides of sick and dying patients—are ignoring what patients and doctors and health care workers are telling them about real world suffering."[6]

Robert L. DuPont, president of the Institute for Behavior and Health in Rockville, Maryland, contends that these charges are untrue. He says there is an abundance of evidence that medical marijuana is harmful. The idea that marijuana is medicine is a myth spread by those trying to legalize it completely, he argues, and is not backed by scientific evidence. "More people need to see 'medical marijuana' for what it is," says DuPont, "a cynical fraud and a cruel hoax."[7]

> **Many believe that the continuing ban on medical marijuana is based more on politics than on reality.**

## Research Needed

According to the federal government, reclassifying marijuana to permit medical use would require research proving its safety and usefulness as a medicine. The government maintains that, to date, no such research exists. According to the FDA, a thorough review has been conducted by the FDA, SAMHSA, and NIDA, concluding that "no animal or human data supported the safety or efficacy of marijuana for general medical use."[8] However, critics charge that the government is unfairly blocking medical marijuana research. According to the Marijuana Policy Project, "The National Institute on Drug Abuse . . . has consistently made it difficult (and often nearly impossible) for researchers to obtain marijuana for their studies. At present, it is effectively impossible to do the sort of large-scale, extremely costly trials required for FDA approval."[9] Government representatives counter that many research requests do not meet FDA's strict standards. Robert J. Meyer, director of the FDA's Office of Drug Evaluation II, Center for Drug Evaluation and Research, explains: "The Department of Health and Human Services (HSS) and FDA support the medical research community who intend to study marijuana," but this study must be "in scientifically valid investigations and well-controlled trials, in-line with the FDA's drug approval process."[10]

## Enforcement of Marijuana Laws

In the United States, punishments for marijuana-related offenses range from small fines to years in jail. Overall, enforcement of marijuana laws has increased in recent years. According to a 2005 study by the Sentencing Project, a Washington-based think tank, between 1990 and 2002 marijuana arrests increased by 113 percent. At the same time, arrests involving other drugs decreased slightly. Researchers found that marijuana arrests now make up nearly half of the 1.5 million drug arrests that occur annually.

Many people believe that marijuana laws are too harsh and are contrary to what most Americans believe to be fair. According to Nadelmann, "Marijuana prohibition is unique among American laws. No other law is both enforced so widely and harshly and yet deemed unnecessary by such a substantial portion of the populace." Nadelmann concludes, "This is clearly an overreaction on the part of the government."[11] Author Eric Schlosser agrees, arguing that marijuana-related offenses incur greater penalties than more serious offenses, even murder: "Those convicted of a marijuana felony, even if they are disabled, can be prohibited from receiving federal welfare payments or food stamps. Convicted murderers and rapists, however, are still eligible for those benefits." He concludes, "Marijuana prohibition [results in] billions of taxpayer dollars down the drain every year; 700,000 people arrested annually; private properties confiscated; and other basic freedoms violated by government agents futilely trying to enforce paternalistic laws."[12]

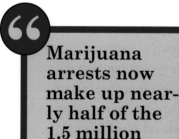

> Marijuana arrests now make up nearly half of the 1.5 million drug arrests that occur annually.

Edmund Hartnett, deputy chief and executive officer of the New York City Police Department Narcotics Division, defends current penalties. He believes that drug users should be punished to deter drug use and the criminal behavior that comes with it. According to Hartnett, the simple reality is that drugs often lead to violence, and many crimes are committed as a result of drug use. An

ONDCP report, "Who's Really in Prison for Marijuana?" counters the belief that current penalties are unnecessarily harsh. It insists that large numbers of people are not spending years in prison simply for personal use of a small amount of marijuana. Instead, "the vast majority of inmates in state and federal prison for marijuana have been found guilty of much more than simple possession," it explains. "Some were convicted for drug trafficking, some for marijuana possession along with one or more other offenses."[13]

> **Regardless of extensive debate over marijuana laws, people continue to use it in societies around the world.**

## The Legalization Debate

In addition to disagreement over marijuana penalties, there is ongoing debate in the United States and elsewhere over whether or not marijuana should be legalized entirely. Nadelmann insists that marijuana prohibition has been a disaster and should be discontinued. "When a government prohibition proves ineffective, unreasonably costly, and substantially more harmful than the supposed evil it was intended to cure, that prohibition merits repeal," he says, "just as alcohol prohibition did 70 years ago."[14] However, NIDA director Nora D. Volkow insists, "Marijuana is not a benign drug. It is illegal and has significant adverse health and social consequences associated with its use."[15] For these reasons, she believes it must remain illegal.

Regardless of extensive debate over marijuana laws, people continue to use it in most societies around the world. In his book, *Hemp—American History Revisited*, Robert Deitch points out that for as long as civilization has existed, marijuana use—as both an intoxicant and a medicine—has been an integral part of many societies and is thus deeply entrenched in these cultures: "Some would argue that we are never going to stop people from using recreational intoxicants [such as marijuana]."[16] One thing is certain: This intoxicant continues to provoke conflict concerning its effects on individual health and on society, and there is fierce debate over whether or not it should be legalized for medical or recreational use. With persuasive support on both sides of these issues, the debate over marijuana is unlikely to be resolved in the near future.

# Is Marijuana Harmful to Health?

> ❝ The *cannabis sativa* plant from which marijuana comes is a complex chemical factory. Marijuana contains 426 known chemicals that are transformed into 2,000 chemicals when burned during the smoking process.❞

—James A. Inciardi, *The War on Drugs III: The Continuing Saga of the Mysteries and Miseries of Intoxication, Addiction, and Public Policy*

Though the amount of research into the therapeutic value of marijuana is disputed, there is abundant data on the physiological and psychological effects of marijuana, including studies, research reviews, polls, and personal reports. However, interpretations of all this information vary widely. While there is a strong case that marijuana has certain harmful biological effects, there are also convincing arguments that marijuana does not harm human health. As journalist Nick Brownlee explains, "There are lies and statistics. . . . And when it comes to an issue as controversial as cannabis, statistics can be found to bolster both sides of the argument."[17] The main topics of concern in relation to marijuana and health are its effect on the respiratory and other bodily systems, how it influences brain activity, whether or not the increased potency of marijuana makes it more toxic or potentially more addictive, and whether it functions as a gateway drug.

## Effects on the Body

One of the biggest causes of controversy is the fact that marijuana is most commonly smoked. Many people believe that the practice of smoking itself makes it harmful to health. Researchers have found that marijuana smoke contains some of the same harmful chemicals as tobacco smoke, and believe that therefore smoking marijuana damages the respiratory system just as tobacco smoke has been proven to do. Sherwood O. Cole, psychologist and author of numerous drug-related articles, states, "Like tobacco, marijuana smoke increases the risk of cancer and lung damage. This should not be surprising since marijuana contains most of the same chemical components (except nicotine) that are found in tobacco."[18] The National Institute on Drug Abuse (NIDA) echoes this position, insisting that "someone who smokes marijuana regularly may have many of the same respiratory problems that tobacco smokers do."[19] In 2006 such widely held beliefs were challenged when pulmonologist Donald Tashkin presented the results of a large study that surprised even those conducting it. Researchers found no association between marijuana use and lung cancer, even in very heavy marijuana users. According to Tashkin, there was even a suggestion of some protective effect of marijuana smoke against lung cancer.

> " Marijuana smoke contains some of the same harmful chemicals as tobacco smoke does. "

A number of research studies have found that marijuana may also be harmful to numerous other parts of the body. According to the Drug Enforcement Administration (DEA), marijuana weakens the immune system, making it more difficult for the body to resist infection. There are studies showing that it is harmful to the cardiovascular system because it raises blood pressure and heart rate. Some researchers believe marijuana also harms the reproductive system, reducing fertility in both males and females. Offsetting these charges, however, is evidence that people can use marijuana for years and experience no such ill effects. Activist David Salyer argues:

> As far back as 1972, a review of the existing scientific evidence about marijuana by the National Commission on Marijuana and Drug Abuse concluded that . . . [marijuana's] dangers had been grossly overstated. Since then, researchers have conducted thousands of studies of humans, animals and cell cultures without government sanction. None reveal any findings dramatically different from those

described by the National Commission in 1972. In 1995, based on thirty years of scientific research, editors of the British medical journal *Lancet* concluded that "the smoking of cannabis, even long-term, is not harmful to health."[20]

## Marijuana and the Brain

Another health aspect that is commonly discussed in relation to marijuana is its effect on the brain. Cole examined numerous studies on the topic and concluded that "the impairment of cognitive performance by cannabis is generally well accepted in the literature."[21] There is broad support for the conclusion that marijuana use can cause cognitive impairments such as a slow reaction time, difficulty concentrating and remembering, and difficulty performing complex tasks. Many argue, though, that these impairments are only temporary and end with use of the drug. The National Center on Addiction and Substance Abuse (CASA) at Columbia University disagrees, finding that cognitive impairment worsens with increasing years of marijuana use. CASA also finds that long-term use can cause harmful changes in the brain similar to those seen after long-term use of other drugs such as cocaine. Contradicting all these findings, however, is a 2003 study in which researchers Raul Gonzalez, Catherine L. Carey, Loki Natarajan, and Tanya Wolfson conclude that in adults, long-term recreational marijuana use had little or no impact on a number of cognitive skills, including reaction time, verbal skills, motor skills, and learning.

> "There is broad support for the conclusion that marijuana use can cause cognitive impairments."

Critics point out that even if marijuana use is safe for a healthy adult, it may be risky for youth, because their brains are still developing, and for pregnant women, because they are carrying a vulnerable fetus, also with developing brain tissue. Many people believe that regular use impedes critical brain development in young people. According to Office of National Drug Control Policy (ONDCP), it also impairs the ability of youth to concentrate and retain information, and is associated with poor performance in school. Such effects mean that teens may not master important academic skills that they need for success later in life. Studies of women who have used marijuana while pregnant show that their children may have a lower birth weight, and may experience difficulty with problem-solving, memory, and attention.

In addition to questions of cognitive impairment, researchers disagree about whether regular marijuana use might be related to the development of mental illness, particularly schizophrenia. A number of studies have found a connection between the two. A 2005 report by the Substance Abuse and Mental Health Services Administration (SAMHSA) states that marijuana use is associated with an increased risk of schizophrenia or other mental illnesses. Another study in the February 2004 issue of the *British Journal of Psychiatry* reports that marijuana doubles the risk of developing schizophrenia. Other researchers believe that marijuana might not actually cause mental illnesses such as schizophrenia, but might make these problems more likely in individuals already predisposed to them.

> " Many people believe that regular [marijuana] use impedes critical brain development in young people. "

In 2005, however, one group of researchers concluded that even this theory might be untrue. Jason Schiffman headed a study testing the relationship between marijuana use and behavior suggestive of schizophrenia. In the majority of individuals, researchers found that such behavior usually existed before marijuana use. Their conclusion is that schizophrenia probably exists before marijuana use occurs, and that a causative link between marijuana and schizophrenia is unlikely.

Further complicating the debate over marijuana's effects on the brain is the fact that recent research has found natural brain chemicals similar to the cannabinoids in marijuana. The brain has receptors for these chemicals—the same receptors used when a person uses marijuana. As a result, some people conclude that marijuana is not harmful because it mimics naturally occurring chemicals and utilizes existing brain connections. NIDA contends that marijuana use is still harmful because it overstimulates these receptors and disrupts their normal function.

## Potency

Anti-marijuana groups frequently assert that one reason marijuana is so harmful to health is that its potency has risen in the past few decades.

According to ONDCP director John Walters, today's marijuana is on average twice as strong as the average marijuana available in the mid-1980s. The ONDCP says that average levels of THC—the main active ingredient in marijuana—rose from less than 1 percent in the mid-1970s to more than 6 percent in 2002. To support the claim that increasing potency means increasing toxicity, critics point to statistics connecting marijuana use with emergency room visits. According to Walters, "Marijuana's role in emergency-room cases has tripled in the past decade."[22] He sees this as a clear indication that increasingly potent marijuana is more dangerous to health than ever before.

> **There has never been a death as a result of a marijuana overdose.**

Opponents argue, however, that such statistics on potency are simply not true and that correlations do not prove a cause-and-effect relationship. In 2004 the European Monitoring Centre for Drugs and Drug Addiction conducted an extensive review of the evidence on marijuana potency in Europe, the United States, Australia, and New Zealand. It concluded, "Statements in the popular media that the potency of cannabis has increased by ten times or more in recent decades are not supported by the limited data that are available from either the USA or Europe."[23] Critics also point out that even if marijuana-related emergency room visits have increased, marijuana is still a relatively safe drug. There has never been a death as a result of a marijuana overdose, they note, while the same cannot be said for some other legal drugs such as aspirin or alcohol.

## Addiction

Today it is generally accepted that marijuana does have the potential to cause addiction. Some people use the drug to the degree that it interferes with normal family, school, and work activities, and researchers have documented various withdrawal symptoms such as irritability, sleeplessness, and anxiety. There is less consensus on how widespread marijuana addiction is in the United States and how serious the problem is. The nonprofit Mayo Clinic calls marijuana addiction a real possibility for marijuana users. According to DEA administrator Karen P. Tandy, marijuana addiction is a serious problem in the United States, particularly for youth. She says that more teens go into treatment for marijuana dependency than for all other drugs combined, including alcohol.

Journalist Dan Gardener points out that it might be misleading to measure addiction by the number of teens entering treatment. He says that many courts allow some individuals charged with drug offenses to avoid jail by entering a treatment program. According to Gardener, almost 60 percent of teen admissions for marijuana treatment are ordered by a judge, meaning that a youth entering a treatment facility may have simply been caught with as little as one marijuana cigarette, or joint, and is not experiencing true addiction. Drug Policy Alliance director Ethan A. Nadelmann echoes Gardener, insisting that "few Americans who enter 'treatment' for marijuana are addicted."[24] He adds that when looking at treatment center admission rates, we must also consider the rate at which the general population uses a particular drug. He believes that one reason more people enter treatment for marijuana than other drugs is the simple fact that millions of Americans smoke marijuana, while far fewer ever use other illicit drugs. Thus, it is logical that even if a relatively small percentage of marijuana users actually become addicted, that percentage may be a larger absolute number.

> " Some people believe that through marijuana use, people are emboldened to . . . try more harmful drugs. "

## The Gateway Theory

Yet another critique of marijuana is that it acts as a gateway drug—one that leads users to try harder drugs such as cocaine or heroin. Some people believe that through marijuana use, people are emboldened to take greater risks and try more harmful drugs, and that people's access to and contact with harder drugs increases simply by buying marijuana from dealers who sell other drugs too. According to Tandy, "In drug law enforcement, rarely do we meet heroin or cocaine addicts who did not start their drug use with marijuana."[25] SAMHSA found evidence that the gateway theory is valid for young people. SAMHSA researchers report that the younger a child is when first using marijuana, the more likely he or she is to use cocaine and heroin, and to become dependent on drugs.

Critics rebut such arguments by pointing out that while some people who use cocaine and heroin have used marijuana first, this does not mean marijuana caused their use. As professor Douglas Husak points out, " In reality . . . few users of marijuana graduate to heavy use of other illicit drugs."[26] In her experience with young patients, psychiatrist Sally Satel found that hard drug use was precipitated by causes other than marijuana. Among the young people she treated, those who progressed from marijuana to hard drugs did so because of problems such as a chaotic home life, depression, problems in school, or alcohol use.

## Continuing Controversy

As researchers and marijuana users continue to generate more evidence on the health effects of marijuana, the debate seems to get more complicated. Prohibitionists continue to insist that marijuana is harmful to the respiratory, cardiovascular, and reproductive systems. They present evidence that it harms the brain and causes mental illness, is increasingly addictive and dangerously potent, and acts as a gateway drug to harder drug use. Marijuana advocates charge that such claims are unfounded, and counter with opposing research showing no harmful effects of marijuana. The health effects of marijuana continue to be a contentious topic.

# Primary Source Quotes*

# Is Marijuana Harmful to Health?

66 **Marijuana harms in many ways, and kids are the most vulnerable to its damaging effects. Use of the drug can lead to significant health . . . , learning or behavioral problems, especially for young users.** 99

—Office of National Drug Control Policy, "Marijuana Myths & Facts: The Truth Behind 10 Popular Misconceptions," November 2004.

The Office of National Drug Control Policy was established in 1988 with the goal of eradicating illicit drug manufacture, sale, and use in the United States. It also works to eliminate drug-related crime, violence, and negative health consequences.

66 **The health risks associated with Marijuana are often exaggerated.** 99

—Marijuana Legalization Organization, "Marijuana and Health," 2006. www.mjlegal.org.

The Marijuana Legalization Organization believes that marijuana prohibition is expensive, harmful, and goes against the idea of a free society. Its members advocate the legalization of marijuana.

* Editor's Note: While the definition of a primary source can be narrowly or broadly defined, for the purposes of Compact Research, a primary source consists of: 1) results of original research presented by an organization or researcher; 2) eyewitness accounts of events, personal experience, or work experience; 3) first-person editorials offering pundits' opinions; 4) government officials presenting political plans and/or policies; 5) representatives of organizations presenting testimony or policy.

&#x66;&#x66;There are numerous deleterious health consequences associated with . . . marijuana use. . . . Those who engage in a lifetime of heavy marijuana use . . . [report] an overall dissatisfaction with their mental and physical health.&#x99;

—Nora D. Volkow, "Marijuana and Medicine: The Need for a Science-Based Approach," testimony before the House Committee on Government Reform, Subcommittee on Criminal Justice, Drug Policy, and Human Resources, April 1, 2004.

Volkow is director of the National Institute on Drug Abuse and an international leader in drug addiction research and brain imaging.

&#x66;&#x66;Most cannabis users do so responsibly and in moderation and risk little in the way of health effects. . . . Use does not necessarily equate with harm.&#x99;

—National Organization for the Reform of Marijuana Laws, New Zealand, "NORML's Submission to the National Drug Policy Consultation," June 9, 2006.

The National Organization for the Reform of Marijuana Laws aims to legalize the responsible use of marijuana by adults. It has chapters in numerous U.S. states and in other countries.

&#x66;&#x66;Marijuana smoke contains 50 percent to 70 percent more carcinogenic hydrocarbons than does tobacco smoke. . . . Marijuana users usually inhale more deeply and hold their breath longer than tobacco smokers do, which increases the lungs' exposure to carcinogenic smoke. These facts suggest that, puff for puff, smoking marijuana may increase the risk of cancer more than smoking tobacco does.&#x99;

—National Institute on Drug Abuse, "Marijuana Abuse," June 2005.

The National Institute on Drug Abuse is part of the U.S. Department of Health and Human Services and works to prevent drug abuse and addiction in the United States.

**❝In my work . . . I find that one drug above all others is prone to precipitate acute mental derangement: cannabis.❞**

—Margaret Cook, "Cannabis: A Bad Trip for the Young," *New Statesman*, January 31, 2005, p. 10.

Cook is a medical doctor and a frequent contributor to the *New Statesman*, a British weekly political magazine.

.......................................................................................................................................................

**❝[My experience] conflicts with supposed marijuana facts. . . . My close associates and I have not suffered any major illnesses since we began using marijuana on a regular basis.❞**

—Emancipated," "A Way of Life," *Dr. Lester Grinspoon's Marijuana Uses*, 2006. www.marijuana-uses.com.

"Emancipated" is the pseudonym of a twenty-six-year-old marijuana user who lives in Canada.

.......................................................................................................................................................

**❝It was as though someone had stolen [my son] overnight. He was talking weirdly, his thoughts were all over the place, he was having hallucinations, and was totally paranoid [as a result of marijuana use].❞**

—BBC News, "Out of Joint," January 20, 2005. http://news.bbc.co.uk.

The unnamed author of this article, published by the British Broadcasting Corporation, describes how marijuana use caused his son to suffer from mental illness.

.......................................................................................................................................................

**❝** Despite widespread concern, there is no strong evidence that use of cannabis has important consequences for psychological . . . health.**❞**

—John Macleod et al., "Psychological and Social Sequelae of Cannabis and Other Illicit Drug Use by Young People: A Systematic Review of Longitudinal, General Population Studies," *Lancet,* May 15, 2004.

Macleod is a senior lecturer for the Department of Primary Care and General Practice at the University of Birmingham, United Kingdom.

---

**❝** In the last 10 years . . . we have seen a nearly 200% increase in the number of emergency room admissions mentions that are attributed to marijuana. . . . That should get our attention that we are facing a risk that we haven't fully apprehended.**❞**

—David Murray, "HB 96: Crimes Involving Marijuana and Other Drugs," testimony before the House Judiciary Committee, April 8, 2005.

Murray is special assistant to the director of the Office of National Drug Control Policy.

---

**❝** There has never been a death attributed to an overdose of marijuana. Clearly, most prescription drugs are far more dangerous than marijuana. Even over-the-counter drugs like aspirin and Tylenol cause numerous overdose deaths each year.**❞**

—Rob Kampia, testimony before the House Committee on Government Reform, Subcommittee on Criminal Justice, Drug Policy, and Human Resources, April 1, 2004. www.maps.org.

Kampia is an activist for marijuana policy reform. He is the founder of the Marijuana Policy Project, an organization that works to remove criminal penalties for marijuana use.

---

66 **Marijuana continues to be a significant threat because today's more potent marijuana causes more teens to be dependent on it. This is supported by . . . [data showing that] more teens seek treatment for marijuana dependency than for all other drugs combined.** 99

—Karen P. Tandy, "Drug Threats and Enforcement Operations," congressional testimony, April 5, 2006.

Tandy is administrator of the Drug Enforcement Administration.

66 **Most marijuana today is only modestly more potent than that remembered wistfully by baby boomers, and there are no grounds for claiming . . . that marijuana today is so much stronger as to be a wholly different drug.** 99

—Dan Gardner, "Is Pot More Potent than in the Past?" *Ottawa Citizen,* March 20, 2005. http://cannabisnews.com.

Gardner is a columnist for the *Ottawa (Ontario) Citizen* newspaper.

66 **The association between the use of marijuana and other drugs is well established. . . . People who use marijuana are at higher risk for using other illegal drugs.** 99

—National Center on Addiction and Substance Abuse at Columbia University, "Non-Medical Marijuana II: Rite of Passage or Russian Roulette?" April 2004.

The National Center on Addiction and Substance Abuse (CASA) at Columbia University focuses on the study of all forms of substance abuse and its effects on society. CASA's staff includes experts from numerous fields including addiction, criminology, public health, sociology, and statistics.

66 **The vast majority of Americans who have tried marijuana have never gone on to try other illegal drugs, much less get into trouble with them.** 99

—Ethan A. Nadelmann, "An End to Marijuana Prohibition: The Drive to Legalize Picks Up," *National Review,* July 12, 2004.

Nadelmann is founder and executive director of the Drug Policy Alliance, an organization promoting drug policy reform and alternatives to the government's war on drugs.

# Is Marijuana Harmful to Health?

- According to the U.S. Drug Enforcement Agency, one marijuana cigarette deposits approximately four times more tar in the lungs than a filtered tobacco cigarette.

- In a 2006 study led by Donald Tashkin, researchers found that people who had smoked more than twenty thousand marijuana joints did not have an increased risk of lung cancer.

- According to the Office of National Drug Control Policy, marijuana use can increase the heart rate by twenty to fifty beats per minute, or even double its normal rate.

- In 2002 and 2003 the National Survey on Drug Use and Health found that 12.5 percent of adults who reported lifetime marijuana use had suffered from a serious mental illness in the past year.

- In 2003 researchers at the University of New South Wales in Sydney found that while marijuana use among Australian teenagers has increased substantially over the past thirty years, there has been no corresponding increase in schizophrenia.

- According to the Office of National Drug Control Policy, average THC levels in marijuana rose from less than 1 percent in the mid-1970s to more than 6 percent in 2002.

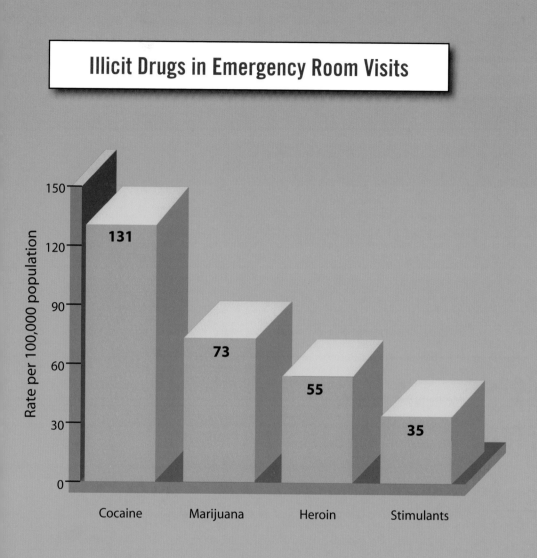

# Illicit Drugs in Emergency Room Visits

**Rate per 100,000 population**

- 131 — Cocaine
- 73 — Marijuana
- 55 — Heroin
- 35 — Stimulants

This graph shows national estimates of 2004 emergency room visits that were related to the use of illicit drugs. Marijuana-related visits were higher than heroin or stimulants, but significantly lower than cocaine-related visits.

Source: Office of Applied Studies, Substance Abuse and Mental Health Services Administration, *Drug Abuse Warning Network*, September 2004. http://dawninfo.samhas.gov.

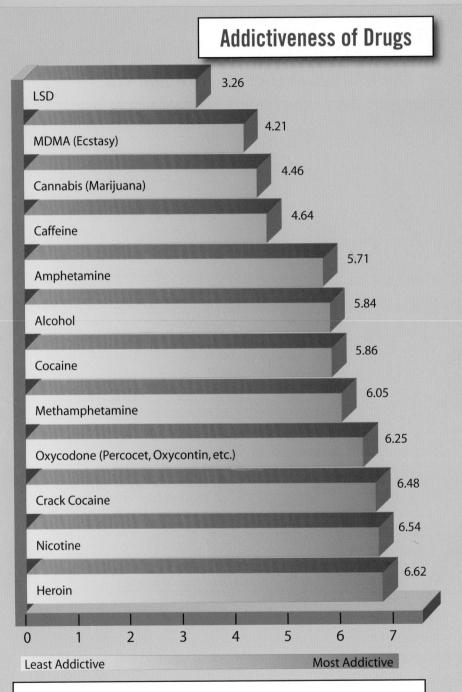

## Addictiveness of Drugs

| Drug | Rating |
|------|--------|
| LSD | 3.26 |
| MDMA (Ecstasy) | 4.21 |
| Cannabis (Marijuana) | 4.46 |
| Caffeine | 4.64 |
| Amphetamine | 5.71 |
| Alcohol | 5.84 |
| Cocaine | 5.86 |
| Methamphetamine | 6.05 |
| Oxycodone (Percocet, Oxycontin, etc.) | 6.25 |
| Crack Cocaine | 6.48 |
| Nicotine | 6.54 |
| Heroin | 6.62 |

Least Addictive      Most Addictive

This chart is derived from experts' subjective ratings of the tolerance, withdrawal, and addiction created by twelve different drugs. It shows that marijuana is significantly less addictive than many other drugs, including alcohol and caffeine.

Source: Robert Gore and Mitch Earleywine, "Addiction Potential of Drugs of Abuse: A Survey of Clinicians and Researchers," Department of Psychology, University of Southern California, October 2004.

According to this data from the U.S. Drug Enforcement Agency, among those entering treatment for substance abuse, 61.9 percent report that marijuana is their primary substance of abuse. Abuse of other types of illicit drugs such as cocaine and opiates were each under 5 percent.

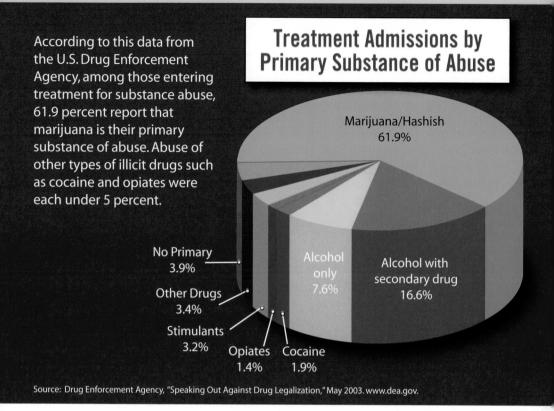

**Treatment Admissions by Primary Substance of Abuse**

Marijuana/Hashish
61.9%

No Primary
3.9%

Other Drugs
3.4%

Stimulants
3.2%

Opiates
1.4%

Cocaine
1.9%

Alcohol only
7.6%

Alcohol with secondary drug
16.6%

Source: Drug Enforcement Agency, "Speaking Out Against Drug Legalization," May 2003. www.dea.gov.

- The National Institute on Drug Abuse reports that marijuana was the third most commonly abused drug mentioned in admission reports of drug-related emergency room visits in the last half of 2003 in the United States.

- According to the National Organization for the Reform of Marijuana Laws, of drug-related emergency room visits that mentioned marijuana in 2002, only 28 percent involved marijuana alone.

- The Office of National Drug Control Policy reports that adults who used marijuana as youth are eight times more likely to have used cocaine and fifteen times more likely to have used heroin.

- In a May 2004 report in the *American Journal of Public Health*, researchers found that decriminalization of marijuana in Amsterdam was not associated with greater use of other illicit drugs there.

# How Does Marijuana Use Affect Society?

> **[Cannabis] will continue to weave its extraordinary influence on us for as long as it finds soil to grow in.**
>
> —Nick Brownlee, *The Complete Illustrated Guide to Cannabis*

One reason for marijuana's illegal status in most countries is that many people believe this drug adversely affects not only users but society as a whole. The Office of National Drug Control Policy (ONDCP) explains this point of view: "[The] use of marijuana . . . comes at a significant expense to society in terms of lost employee productivity, public health care costs, and accidents."[27] Others believe, however, that marijuana primarily affects only the person using it and that adults should be able to make their own decisions about whether or not to use this drug. Journalist Alan Young points out that marijuana use is like many other activities that involve an element of risk and should not be prohibited on that basis: "Even flush toilets and articles of clothing can wreak havoc," he says:

> Studies show that 40,000 Americans injure themselves on their toilet seats every year, and 100,000 are injured by their clothing annually. . . . We accept and tolerate these risks because we believe there is social utility in having flush toilets [and] clothing. . . . Yet when it comes to marijuana, we seem unwilling to tolerate any level of risk.[28]

The risks of marijuana use in society include its potential to cause violent behavior, crime, and automobile accidents; its possible relationship to risky sexual behavior; and its possible inhibitory effect on educational and workplace achievement and social interaction. Society continues to disagree over the seriousness of these risks, and whether they justify marijuana's prohibition.

## Violent Behavior and Crime

Many critics of marijuana charge that it promotes violence. According to the ONDCP, "Research shows a link between frequent marijuana use and increased violent behavior."[29] The agency reports, "Young people who use marijuana weekly are nearly four times more likely than nonusers to engage in violence."[30] Edmund Hartnett, deputy chief and executive officer of the New York City Police Department Narcotics Division, insists that violence and crime are an inextricable part of drug use. When people's minds are altered by drugs—including marijuana—they are much more likely to commit crimes, he says. The U.S. Drug Enforcement Administration (DEA) agrees.

> **Many critics of marijuana charge that it promotes violence.**

It states, "Crime, violence and drug use go hand in hand. . . . Most drug crimes aren't committed by people trying to pay for drugs; they're committed by people on drugs."[31]

But marijuana advocates such as Sheryl Jackson-Sczbecki contend that this is not the case. While there is a connection between, for example, alcohol intoxication or hallucinogenic drugs and violent behavior, marijuana merely provides a relaxing high, says Jackson-Sczbecki: "Marijuana does not make you want to punch out your boss, your mate or physically and sexually abuse your children. Marijuana does not allow one to be hateful and rude to those who care for you, and seldom does one have to apologize for one's unruly and often obnoxious behavior."[32] Medical anthropologist Merrill Singer agrees that marijuana use does not seem to be a major cause of violence. According to Singer, "Of all the psychoactive drugs, violence is most commonly associated with alcohol consumption."[33]

Another common argument made by marijuana critics is that marijuana causes crime. They cite statistics showing a correlation between marijuana use and criminal behavior. According to the ONDCP, approximately

30 percent of federal prisoners used marijuana or hashish in the month before their arrest, and 11 percent had used it at the time of their offense. Thirty-nine percent of state prisoners used it in the month before their arrest, 15 percent at the time of their offense. Anti-drug organization Just Think Twice reports that the percentage of youth engaging in delinquent behaviors such as fighting, stealing, or selling illegal drugs tends to increase with marijuana use. The Substance Abuse and Mental Health Services Administration (SAMHSA) also found that frequent marijuana use is associated with delinquent behaviors among youth. It reports that the percentage of youth engaging in delinquent behaviors rises with increasing frequency of marijuana use.

> [Some people believe that the] cause of crime is not marijuana, but alcohol.

The National Organization for the Reform of Marijuana Laws (NORML) maintains, however, that the crime rate is actually higher than it would be if marijuana were legalized. As the New Zealand branch of NORML explains, "Prohibition raises the price of addictive drugs and forces users to commit property crime which would not be necessary if drugs were legally available."[34] Singer believes the major substance-abuse cause of crime is not marijuana, but alcohol. He cites a study in which researchers investigated two hundred sixty-eight people who had been arrested for homicide. They found that one-third had used marijuana on the day of their crime; however, most of these offenders were also under the influence of alcohol.

## Automobile Accidents

Those in favor of marijuana prohibition also argue that marijuana harms society by contributing to automobile accidents. According to a 2004 report by the National Center on Addiction and Substance Abuse (CASA) at Columbia University, driving under the influence of marijuana is dangerous. CASA states that marijuana impairs drivers' coordination and reaction time. While many people believe this drug allows them to drive responsibly, this is a myth, says CASA: "Second only to alcohol, marijuana is the drug most detected in impaired drivers, fatally injured drivers and motor vehicle crash victims."[35] Data from the National Highway Traffic Safety Administration (NHTSA) support CASA's finding. Among those involved in traffic arrests and fatalities, the most frequently detected psychoactive substance is marijuana, according to NHTSA.

However, opponents argue that, as with marijuana-crime correlations, traffic statistics blaming marijuana use are often confounded by alcohol abuse. According to marijuana advocate Mitch Earleywine, many drivers who are reportedly under the influence of marijuana when they have an accident are also under the influence of alcohol: "Alcohol really contributes to driving problems and those get neglected when we're sometimes interpreting data."[36]

According to Earleywine, marijuana alone does not significantly impact driving ability. He cites studies from the Netherlands on driving under the influence of marijuana, in which researchers found that people under the influence of marijuana were still competent drivers. He says, "[Drivers] show no impairment in their turning, in their ability to follow another car, they tend to slow down, they increase their stopping distance, they increase the distance between their car and the car in front of them and they're actually very safe along those domains."[37]

## Marijuana and Sexual Behavior

Driving ability is not the only behavior that concerns opponents of marijuana; some also are concerned about how marijuana influences sexual behavior, especially in young people. They believe that it reduces inhibitions and its users are more likely to engage in unsafe sex, and more likely to contract sexually transmitted diseases. According to Just Think Twice, marijuana use is related to risky behaviors, including having multiple sex partners. Some experts cite strong evidence between drug use, including marijuana use, unsafe sex, and the spread of HIV. Jackson-Sczbecki disagrees with such conclusions. She believes that marijuana does not cause users to lose control or engage in sexual behavior that they will regret later: "It does not cause moral decay nor does it make you want to bed strangers."[38] In her opinion, marijuana users remain in control of their behavior, including sexual behavior.

> " [Critics of marijuana] believe that . . . its users are more likely to engage in unsafe sex. "

# Educational Achievement

Critics of marijuana also charge that it decreases motivation and achievement, particularly among youth. The National Institute on Drug Abuse (NIDA) finds, for example, that "because marijuana compromises the ability to learn and remember information, the more a person uses marijuana the more he or she is likely to fall behind in accumulating intellectual, job, or social skills."[39] NIDA reports that students who use marijuana are negatively affected because they get lower grades and are less likely to graduate from high school than those who do not use marijuana. It also finds negative consequences among adults in the workplace: "Workers who smoke marijuana are more likely than their co-workers to have problems on the job. Several studies associated workers' marijuana smoking with increased absences, tardiness, accidents, workers' compensation claims, and job turnover."[40] SAMHSA echoes these findings, asserting that people who use marijuana daily are more likely to be unemployed than people who do not use marijuana or who use it less than daily. In 2005 congressional testimony, physician El Sohly explained such observations with what he calls an antimotivational syndrome that occurs when people use marijuana. "They don't want to do much," he says. "They don't want to be involved, they don't want to be social, they have the tendency to want to be by themselves are not really motivated to do anything at all."[41]

> The National Institute on Drug Abuse . . . . reports that students who use marijuana are . . . less likely to graduate from high school.

Others maintain, on the contrary, that marijuana does not lead to unemployment and failure, and that it is possible to use marijuana and function as a normal, productive member of society. According to marijuana advocate Tasha H. Bangor, "While under the influence of marijuana, you have full awareness as to what is going on in your surroundings. You are able to be a completely responsible parent and proficient at school or work." She adds, "The children of marijuana . . . users do not even have to know that their parents are using drugs."[42] Some people offer another explanation for the relationship between marijuana and negative school and workplace behavior. They argue that marijuana use is simply a manifestation of psychological problems. They believe that certain people are predisposed to antisocial behavior and reduced intellectual achievement, and also to marijuana use. A May 2004 study reported in the British medical journal *Lancet* lends support to this theory. Researchers reviewed forty-eight studies on marijuana use by young people. They found associations between marijuana use and both lower educational attainment and increased reported use of other illicit drugs. However, they did not find much evidence for marijuana use actually causing lower educational achievement or other drug use. They concluded that preexisting psychological problems caused both the marijuana use and these other problems.

## Social Interaction

Some people believe marijuana actually helps them to function better in society. For example, an anonymous writer on marijuana activist Lester Grinspoon's *Marijuana Uses* Web site maintains that regular marijuana use has helped him overcome social anxiety and depression and allows him to participate fully in society: "This is not some harmful illicit substance but rather a natural miracle that has allowed me to take control of myself and start living life."[43] James Inciardi, director of the Center for Drug and Alcohol Studies at the University of Delaware, argues that claims such as this are misguided. While many people believe that marijuana improves their awareness and relationships with others, says Inciardi, in reality, "Marijuana serves as a buffer . . . enabling users to tolerate problems rather than face them."[44]

## A Significant Impact

Author Robert Deitch suggests that there is more to the debate over the societal effects of marijuana than its role in problems such as crime, traffic accidents, and sexually transmitted diseases. In his opinion, marijuana is not prohibited simply to protect society from its potentially harmful effects. In fact, says Deitch, some sectors of society actually benefit from marijuana's illegal status. He suggests that if marijuana became legal, sales of marijuana would reduce the profits of

> Many people believe that marijuana improves their awareness and relationships with others.

pharmaceutical companies and liquor and tobacco manufacturers, whose products would face stiff new competition in the marketplace. Says Deitch, "The only reason for the 'war on drugs' is to keep Cannabis illegal, as a favor to corporate America—specifically the . . . liquor and tobacco industries . . . and especially the pharmaceutical companies."[45] While Deitch's charges are unproven, they underscore the fact that marijuana does have a significant impact on society. The nature of that impact is a cause of controversy, and critics continue to argue about how marijuana use relates to violence and crime, driving behavior, sexual activity, education and workplace achievement, and social interaction. And, as Deitch reveals, they also argue about who might benefit from marijuana prohibition. Directly and indirectly, though, marijuana does influence private activity and public policy.

# How Does Marijuana Use Affect Society?

❝Law enforcement professionals . . . work every day with criminals and we know the damage marijuana and other drugs do in our society. . . . The argument that violent criminals don't smoke marijuana is just ludicrous.❞

—Richard Perkins, "Do NOT Rock the Ganja!" *Las Vegas City Life*, May 25, 2006.

Perkins is speaker of the Nevada Assembly and chief of police for the city of Henderson, Nevada.

❝Research suggests that among youths, frequency of marijuana use is associated with . . . problem behaviors. . . . In 2002, approximately 21 percent of youths . . . engaged in serious fighting at school or work. . . . The percentages of youths engaging in delinquent behaviors was higher among past year marijuana users than among those who had not used marijuana.❞

—Substance Abuse and Mental Health Services Administration, "Marijuana Use and Delinquent Behaviors Among Youth," January 9, 2004.

The Substance Abuse and Mental Health Services Administration is an agency of the U.S. Department of Health and Human Services. It works to ensure that people with, or at risk for, a mental or addictive disorder have the opportunity for a fulfilling life.

* Editor's Note: While the definition of a primary source can be narrowly or broadly defined, for the purposes of Compact Research, a primary source consists of: 1) results of original research presented by an organization or researcher; 2) eyewitness accounts of events, personal experience, or work experience; 3) first-person editorials offering pundits' opinions; 4) government officials presenting political plans and/or policies; 5) representatives of organizations presenting testimony or policy.

66 There is little direct evidence of a direct link between marijuana use and criminal behavior. . . . Although marijuana use has been increasing at a modest but steady rate since the early 1990s, the crime rate has plummeted. 99

—James Austin, "Rethinking the Consequences of Decriminalizing Marijuana," *National Organization for the Reform of Marijuana Laws*, November 2, 2005.

Austin is president of the JFA Institute, a research center that conducts research on the causes of crime and the justice system's response to crime and offenders. Formerly he was director of the Institute on Crime, Justice, and Corrections at George Washington University in Washington, D.C.

66 You're going to hear quite a few stories about individual cases where somebody may have used cannabis and been involved in an aggressive act, but I want to emphasize that the laboratory research suggests that cannabis does not cause aggression. 99

—Mitch Earleywine, "HB 96: Crimes Involving Marijuana and Other Drugs," testimony before the House Judiciary Committee, April 8, 2005.

Medical marijuana advocate Mitch Earleywine is an associate professor of psychology at the State University of New York at Albany. He has written more than fifty publications on drug use and abuse and is the author of the book *Understanding Marijuana*.

66 Despite evidence of the relationship between marijuana use and road accidents, many people still consider it a safe practice. . . . This is an untenable position: . . . [A marijuana] impaired driver is a dangerous driver. 99

—National Center on Addiction and Substance Abuse at Columbia University, "Non-Medical Marijuana II: Rite of Passage or Russian Roulette?" April 2004.

The National Center on Addiction and Substance Abuse (CASA) at Columbia University focuses on the study of all forms of substance abuse and its effects on society. CASA's staff includes experts from numerous fields including addiction, criminology, public health, sociology, and statistics.

66 **Contrary to the false alarms sounded by public officials, marijuana is not significantly responsible for vehicular carnage.** 99

—Alan Young, "And Marijuana for All," *Now Magazine Online Edition*, April 7–13, 2005. www.nowtoronto.com.

Young teaches law at Osgoode Hall Law School and criminology at the University of Toronto. His work contributed to the establishment of Canada's first medical marijuana program.

66 **Students who smoke marijuana get lower grades and are less likely to graduate from high school, compared with their nonsmoking peers.** 99

—National Institute on Drug Abuse, "InfoFacts: Marijuana," April 2006. www.nida.nih.gov.

The National Institute on Drug Abuse is part of the U.S. Department of Health and Human Services, and works to prevent drug abuse and addiction in the United States. The organization supports research studies on abuse and addiction, and works to educate the public about the results of this research.

66 **Older teenagers who experiment with marijuana generally function as well as nonusers with respect to school and mental well-being.** 99

—Sally Satel, "A Whiff of 'Reefer Madness' in U.S. Drug Policy," *New York Times*, August 16, 2005, p. F6.

Satel is a practicing psychiatrist and a resident scholar at the American Enterprise Institute for Public Policy in Washington, D.C.

66 **For many years, illegal drug use has been a serious problem facing our country. Drugs cost people their savings and their health, and rob children of their promise.** 99

—George W. Bush, radio address, February 28, 2004.

66 **My addiction [to marijuana] has truly handicapped me from being social at all and having the desire to work.** 99

—"Dreamscape," "Time to Quit Marijuana," *Uncommon Knowledge*, April 2, 2006. www.uncommonforum.com.

"Dreamscape" is an anonymous contributor to an online forum for people trying to quit marijuana use.

**❝I'm a marijuana user. I've used it for eight years. During this time, I've excelled in a lot of aspects of life.❞**

—Aaron Mattley, "HB 96: Crimes Involving Marijuana and Other Drugs," testimony before the House Judiciary Committee, April 8, 2005. www.law.state.ak.us.

Mattley, a resident of Alaska, believes that marijuana should be legalized and regulated by the government.

**❝We need to put to rest the thought that there is such a thing as a lone drug user, a person whose habits affect only himself or herself. . . . Marijuana use . . . is not a victimless crime.❞**

—Karen P. Tandy, "Marijuana: The Myths Are Killing Us," *Police Chief*, March 2005. http://policechiefmagazine.org.

Tandy is administrator of the Drug Enforcement Administration.

**❝Despite its reputation as the herb of peace and love . . . marijuana and violence go hand in hand. Marijuana trafficking is a big, violent business.❞**

—Office of National Drug Control Policy, "Marijuana Myths & Facts: The Truth Behind 10 Popular Misconceptions," November 2004.

The Office of National Drug Control Policy was established in 1988 with the goal of eradicating illicit drug manufacture, sale, and use in the United States. It also works to eliminate drug-related crime, violence, and negative health consequences.

**❝As recreational drugs go, marijuana is about as benign as you can get. . . . It does not cause violence. . . . Dangerously impaired people tend to sit still or fall asleep.❞**

—Roedy Green, "Legalising Marijuana," *Canadian Mind Products*, March 15, 2006. http://mindprod.com.

Green is a Canadian computer programmer and creator of the Web site *Canadian Mind Products*, an advocacy site for the rights of plants and animals.

# How Does Marijuana Use Affect Society?

- In 2004 the National Institute on Drug Abuse found that 14.6 million Americans age twelve and older had used marijuana at least once in the month prior to being surveyed.

- According to the National Institute on Drug Abuse, in 2004 about six thousand people a day used marijuana for the first time; 63.8 percent of those were under age eighteen.

- According to the 2005 Monitoring the Future study, 16.5 percent of eighth-graders, 34.1 percent of tenth-graders, and 44.8 percent of twelfth-graders have used marijuana.

- The National Center on Addiction and Substance Abuse at Columbia University reports that nearly 40 percent of teens say they could buy marijuana within a day.

- According to the National Survey on Drug Use and Health, in 2003, 56.9 percent of marijuana users obtained the drug free or shared someone else's marijuana.

- Americans spend more than $10.4 billion every year on marijuana, according to Drug Enforcement Administration administrator Karen P. Tandy.

# Marijuana

This chart shows marijuana use by selected age and race categories. It reveals that approximately half of marijuana users are under age twenty-six, and that males account for about 60 percent of all users. It also shows that the majority of marijuana users are white.

## Marijuana Use by Age, Race, and Gender

| Total Age | White | Black | Indian | Pacific | Asian | Multi-Racial | Hispanic | Total |
|---|---|---|---|---|---|---|---|---|
| 13 | 111,247 | 21,603 | 3,714 | 0 | 4,646 | 3,022 | 44,095 | 188,327 |
| 14 | 360,652 | 43,516 | 7,870 | 78 | 2,861 | 12,440 | 91,676 | 519,093 |
| 15 | 578,280 | 87,487 | 9,143 | 3,151 | 7,980 | 11,662 | 124,099 | 821,802 |
| 16 | 721,450 | 129,803 | 18,829 | 1,293 | 28,179 | 15,401 | 133,993 | 1,048,946 |
| 17 | 924,394 | 148,928 | 7,658 | 1,137 | 7,519 | 24,556 | 160,821 | 1,275,012 |
| 18 | 985,509 | 145,450 | 15,542 | 14,251 | 39,843 | 30,262 | 178,910 | 1,409,766 |
| 19 | 1,047,104 | 150,643 | 17,160 | 1,301 | 33,385 | 38,405 | 137,588 | 1,425,586 |
| 20 | 924,019 | 152,751 | 6,537 | 934 | 41,486 | 25,429 | 141,987 | 1,293,143 |
| 21 | 955,343 | 174,369 | 18,252 | 12,865 | 17,912 | 28,194 | 202,004 | 1,408,939 |
| 22–23 | 1,481,980 | 263,575 | 25,285 | 13,614 | 44,780 | 36,630 | 291,159 | 2,157,023 |
| 24–25 | 1,073,446 | 201,128 | 7,007 | 3,715 | 38,985 | 24,091 | 178,064 | 1,526,435 |
| 26–29 | 1,724,690 | 463,840 | 10,376 | 4,319 | 14,594 | 18,702 | 280,872 | 2,517,392 |
| 30–34 | 1,708,742 | 347,314 | 9,706 | 12,465 | 57,027 | 37,424 | 295,228 | 2,467,904 |
| 35–49 | 4,665,592 | 993,564 | 28,839 | 0 | 20,940 | 83,257 | 351,442 | 6,143,634 |
| 50–64 | 1,260,621 | 182,597 | 23,280 | 3,328 | 0 | 0 | 8,198 | 1,478,022 |
| 65+ | 117,409 | 12,552 | 0 | 0 | 0 | 71,440 | 0 | 201,401 |
| All Ages | 18,680,083 | 3,523,397 | 210,866 | 72,639 | 360,137 | 460,915 | 2,628,050 | 25,936,087 |

| Young Males | White | Black | Indian | Pacific | Asian | Multi-Racial | Hispanic | Total |
|---|---|---|---|---|---|---|---|---|
| 12 | 20,012 | 2,697 | 0 | 0 | 0 | 0 | 5,551 | 28,260 |
| 13 | 49,563 | 12,154 | 2,346 | 0 | 4,646 | 2,750 | 34,012 | 105,471 |
| 14 | 163,630 | 20,289 | 3,839 | 0 | 0 | 6,053 | 58,212 | 252,023 |
| 15 | 309,408 | 34,248 | 6,824 | 2,653 | 2,943 | 9,254 | 54,906 | 420,236 |
| 16 | 369,033 | 78,341 | 4,203 | 766 | 9,160 | 4,974 | 64,562 | 531,038 |
| 17 | 506,110 | 89,438 | 2,643 | 172 | 3,864 | 7,672 | 87,617 | 697,515 |
| 18 | 570,488 | 88,346 | 7,476 | 12,125 | 18,546 | 22,480 | 92,093 | 811,555 |
| 19 | 545,669 | 82,301 | 3,764 | 829 | 19,286 | 18,075 | 99,727 | 769,652 |
| 20 | 517,451 | 91,246 | 4,846 | 0 | 23,235 | 20,017 | 106,640 | 763,436 |
| All | 11,100,019 | 2,287,570 | 114,876 | 53,246 | 151,867 | 307,765 | 1,575,700 | 15,591,043 |

| Young Females | White | Black | Indian | Pacific | Asian | Multi-Racial | Hispanic | Total |
|---|---|---|---|---|---|---|---|---|
| 12 | 19,594 | 1,583 | 1,672 | 190 | 0 | 0 | 2,363 | 25,401 |
| 13 | 61,685 | 9,448 | 1,367 | 0 | 0 | 272 | 10,083 | 82,856 |
| 14 | 197,022 | 23,227 | 4,030 | 78 | 2,861 | 6,387 | 33,464 | 267,070 |
| 15 | 268,872 | 53,239 | 2,319 | 498 | 5,037 | 2,409 | 69,193 | 401,567 |
| 16 | 352,417 | 51,462 | 14,626 | 527 | 19,018 | 10,427 | 69,431 | 517,908 |
| 17 | 418,285 | 59,490 | 5,015 | 965 | 3,655 | 16,884 | 73,204 | 577,497 |
| 18 | 415,021 | 57,103 | 8,065 | 2,125 | 21,296 | 7,782 | 86,818 | 598,211 |
| 19 | 501,434 | 68,342 | 13,396 | 472 | 14,099 | 20,329 | 37,861 | 655,934 |
| 20 | 406,568 | 61,505 | 1,691 | 934 | 18,250 | 5,411 | 35,347 | 529,707 |
| All | 7,580,064 | 1,235,827 | 95,990 | 19,393 | 208,270 | 153,150 | 1,052,350 | 10,345,044 |

Source: Jon B. Gettman, "Crimes of Indiscretion: Marijuana Arrests in the United States," National Organization for the Reform of Marijuana Laws, 2005. www.norml.org.

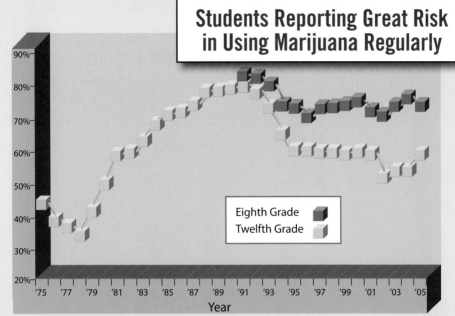

## Students Reporting Great Risk in Using Marijuana Regularly

Source: Centers for Disease Control and Prevention, Youth Risk Behavior Surveillance-United States, June 2006. www.cdc.gov.

Eighth Grade

Twelfth Grade

According to this graph, the majority of students believe there is great risk in using marijuana regularly. For eighth graders, that percentage decreased substantially between 1991 and 1993, and since then has remained at about 75 percent. Among twelfth graders there was also a substantial decrease, and the percentage who currently see great risk in marijuana use is currently just under 60 percent.

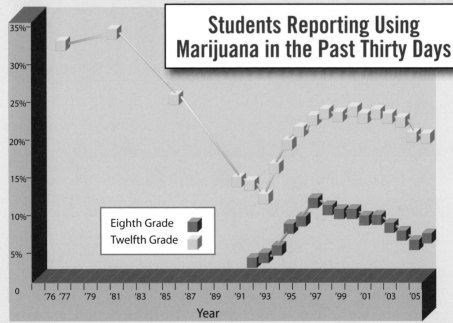

## Students Reporting Using Marijuana in the Past Thirty Days

Source: Child Trends original analysis of Monitoring the Future, 2005 www.childtrendsdatabank.org.

Eighth Grade

Twelfth Grade

The following graph shows marijuana use by eighth and twelfth graders between 1976 and 2005. While use has fluctuated substantially over the past several decades, there has been a slow, steady decline in the past ten years. According to the graph, marijuana use by eighth graders was at 11.3 percent in 1996 and has decreased to only 6.6 percent in 2006. Twelfth grade use declined from 23.6 percent in 1997 to 19.8 percent in 2005.

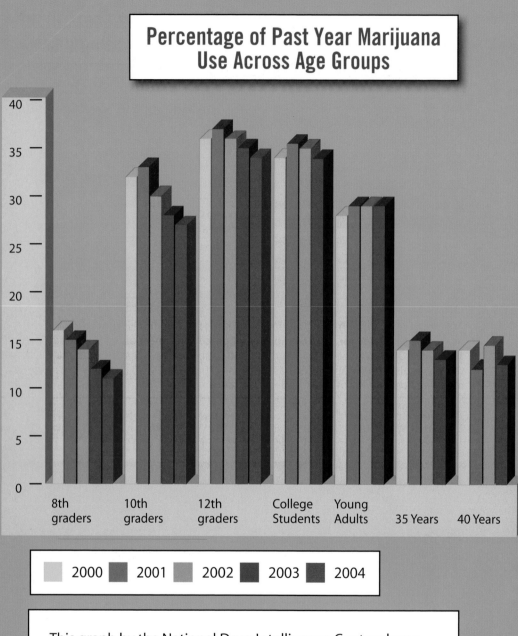

## Percentage of Past Year Marijuana Use Across Age Groups

Legend: 2000, 2001, 2002, 2003, 2004

8th graders · 10th graders · 12th graders · College Students · Young Adults · 35 Years · 40 Years

This graph by the National Drug Intelligence Center shows that marijuana use among eighth, tenth, and twelfth graders as well as college students has declined since 2000. Adult use has changed little.

Source: National Drug Intelligence Center, "National Drug Threat Assessment 2005," February 2005. www.usdoj.gov.

## Marijuana Use by Arrestees, by Gender, 2003

| Past Marijuana Use by Arrestees | Males | Females |
|---|---|---|
| Used in past seven days | 39.3% | 30% |
| Used in past thirty days | 44.9% | 36% |
| Used in past year | 51.9% | 44.4% |
| Avg. # of days used in past thirty days | 10.5 days | 9.1 days |

This chart by the Office of National Drug Control Policy shows marijuana use by both males and females arrested for crimes in the United States. According to the chart, more than one-third of both males and females had used marijuana in the thirty days before their arrest. Males were more likely than females to have used marijuana prior to committing a crime.

Source: Office of National Drug Control Policy, "Drug Facts: Marijuana," February 27, 2006. www.whitehousedrugpolicy.gov.

- According to the Office of National Drug Control Policy, in a 2005 survey of twelfth-graders, only 58 percent categorized smoking marijuana regularly as a "great risk."

- In 2003 the Arrestee Drug Abuse Monitoring Program found that approximately 44 percent of male arrestees and 31 percent of female arrestees tested positive for marijuana at the time of arrest.

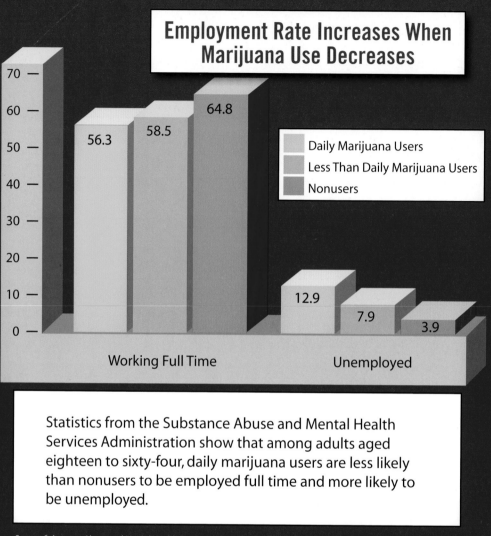

## Employment Rate Increases When Marijuana Use Decreases

Daily Marijuana Users
Less Than Daily Marijuana Users
Nonusers

70

60

50

40

30

20

10

0

56.3    58.5    64.8

Working Full Time

12.9    7.9    3.9

Unemployed

Statistics from the Substance Abuse and Mental Health Services Administration show that among adults aged eighteen to sixty-four, daily marijuana users are less likely than nonusers to be employed full time and more likely to be unemployed.

Source: Substance Abuse and Mental Health Services Administration, "Daily Marijuana Users," *The NSDUH Report,* November 26, 2004.

- According to the National Center on Addiction and Substance Abuse at Columbia University, 56 percent of drivers over the age of sixteen believe that driving within two hours of using marijuana does not make their driving less safe.

- According to the National Institute on Drug Abuse, a study of postal workers found that those using marijuana had 85 percent more injuries than those who tested negative for marijuana use.

# Should Medical Marijuana Be Legal?

**"If cannabis were unknown, and bioprospectors were suddenly to find it in some remote mountain crevice, its discovery would no doubt be hailed as a medical breakthrough. . . . In reality . . . any suggestion that the plant might be medically useful is politically controversial."**

—*Economist*, April 27, 2006

In the United States, there is widespread public support for the use of marijuana in medical treatment. A November 1, 2005, Gallup poll found that 78 percent of Americans support making marijuana legally available for medical prescription. In its "Medical Marijuana Briefing Paper," the Marijuana Policy Project maintains that such results are common. "For over a decade," the group comments, "Polls have consistently shown between 60% and 80% support for legal access to medical marijuana."[46] Medical marijuana remains illegal in the United States, yet as these percentages show, it is an issue that refuses to disappear from public debate. Legalization advocates wrangle with critics over the medical value of marijuana, the effects of smoking it, whether legal alternatives are a good replacement, and the impact that allowing medical marijuana might have on society.

## The Institute of Medicine Study

In the debate over medical marijuana, one research study is widely cited. This 1999 study was commissioned by the White House Office of National Drug Control Policy (ONDCP) and conducted by the Institute of Medicine (IOM), one of the research centers in the federal National

Institutes of Health. IOM researchers found that marijuana might have potential medical value for the terminally ill or patients with debilitating symptoms that do not respond to other drugs. According to John A. Benson Jr., one of the principal investigators, "For these patients, we found that cannabinoids appear to hold potential for treating pain, chemotherapy-induced nausea and vomiting, and the poor appetite and wasting caused by AIDS or advanced cancer."[47]

> [A 1999 Institute of Medicine report concluded] that further scientific research should be conducted to get a better understanding of medical marijuana.

There is extensive debate about the meaning of such statements. Medical marijuana advocates use them to support their cause. For example, Rob Kampia, executive director of the Marijuana Policy Project, sees the IOM study as recognition of marijuana's medical benefits. The *Harvard Health Letter* also interprets the report as a qualified medical endorsement for short-term use of smoked marijuana. Karen P. Tandy, administrator of the U.S. Drug Enforcement Administration (DEA), disagrees. She concedes that the IOM study did suggest the potential of marijuana-based medicines for chronically ill patients. However, she insists that it did not endorse marijuana in its natural form for medical use. She says, "Advocates of medical marijuana frequently tout this study, but the study's findings decisively undercut their arguments. In truth, the IOM explicitly found that marijuana is not medicine. . . . The IOM further found that there was no scientific evidence that smoked marijuana had medical value, even for the chronically ill."[48] Legislation specialist Mark Eddy offers a reason for such conflicting interpretations. "For the most part, the IOM report straddled the issue," he explains, "providing sound bites for both sides of the medical marijuana debate."[49] In his opinion, the main conclusion of the report was that further scientific research should be conducted to get a better understanding of medical marijuana.

## Smoking Medicine

As Tandy's statement on medical marijuana reveals, much of the disapproval of this drug is related to the fact that users usually smoke it. Critics charge that smoking makes it impossible to administer precise doses of a drug, and that it damages lung and other respiratory tissues. According to the Drug Free America Foundation, "Smoking is a poor way to deliver medicine. It is difficult to administer safe, regulated doses of medicines in smoked form. Secondly, the harmful chemicals and carcinogens that are by-products of smoking create entirely new health problems."[50] Addiction specialist Robert L. DuPont agrees. "Burning leaves is not a modern drug delivery system, period," he says. "'Medical marijuana' is an oxymoron."[51]

Yet medical marijuana advocates insist that for those people experiencing debilitating pain or suffering from incurable illnesses, the relief marijuana offers is worth the risk of smoking it. Former U.S. surgeon general Joycelyn Elders agrees: "The evidence is overwhelming that marijuana can relieve certain types of pain, nausea, vomiting and other symptoms caused by illnesses such as multiple sclerosis, cancer and AIDS—or by the harsh drugs sometimes used to treat them. And it can do so with remarkable safety." In her opinion, "For many who need only a small amount—such as cancer patients trying to get through a few months of chemotherapy—the risks of smoking are minor."[52] Physician Kate Scannell concurs: "Almost every sick and dying patient I've ever known who's tried medical marijuana experienced a kinder death."[53]

> **Medical marijuana advocates insist that . . . the relief marijuana offers is worth the risk of smoking it.**

## A Step Toward Overall Legalization?

Another critique of the medical marijuana lobby is that it will not be satisfied with the legalization of marijuana for medical purposes. Critics charge that medical marijuana is simply an important first step in a continuing drive to achieve legalization not only of marijuana but of other illicit substances. The Drug Free America Foundation warns, "It is important to realize that the campaign to allow marijuana to be used as medicine is a tactical maneuver in an overall strategy to completely legalize all drugs." The foundation explains:

> Of those leading the legalization movement, some are
> political activists who have been wanting it legal since the

70s and are now claiming its medical benefits, and others are commodities traders who use their millions to fund initiative movements in states they do not even live in.[54]

Legalization advocate Ethan Nadelmann disagrees:

> If you look at the people who vote for the medical marijuana initiatives in California and other states, roughly half of them support the broader legalization of marijuana and half do not. If you look at the people who put up a lot of the money for these ballot initiatives or these legislative lobbying efforts, similarly, some of them support voter legalization, others do not.[55]

## Legal Alternatives

Some alternatives to medical marijuana already exist. Marinol is a synthetic form of THC (delta-9-tetrahydrocannabinol), the main active ingredient in marijuana, that is legally prescribed in the United States. Sativex is an under-the-tongue cannabis spray available in Canada. Groups such as the Drug Free America Foundation point to these drugs as proof that the chronically ill do not need marijuana. According to the foundation, "Marijuana has no medical value that cannot be met more effectively by the legal, FDA-approved prescription drug Marinol."[56] The DEA concurs: "The Food and Drug Administration has determined that Marinol is safe, effective, and has therapeutic benefits for use as a treatment for nausea and vomiting associated with cancer chemotherapy, and as a treatment of weight loss in patients with AIDS."[57] Psychologist Sherwood O. Cole is one of many people who believe that if medical marijuana has any future, it will be in the form of such drugs. He says, "Undoubtedly, the future of the growing medical use of cannabinoids depends on the development of pure drugs, where the consistency of content, purity, and potency of the product can be carefully controlled."[58]

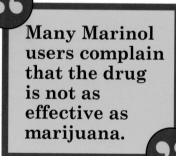

> Many Marinol users complain that the drug is not as effective as marijuana.

Some of those who use synthetic cannabis–based drugs do not support such an optimistic assessment, though. Many Marinol users complain that the drug is not as effective as marijuana and is costly to use. They also complain that unlike marijuana, Marinol gives the user a high that is unpleasant and during which it is difficult to function. According to an editorial in the *National Review*, "Swallowing Marinol takes longer to work, is more expensive, and has more adverse side effects than smoking marijuana."[59]

Some people believe that the effectiveness of marijuana depends on its complex chemical composition, comprising hundreds of chemicals, including nearly seventy different cannabinoids, whose interactions are not scientifically understood. They argue that such a composition, and therefor such effectiveness, is impossible to duplicate in a synthetic drug. Teacher Alan Young warns, "It is a mistake to rely upon laboratory creations and ignore the benefits of a naturally occurring plant."[60]

## Possible Impacts of Allowing Medical Use

Medical marijuana opponents also worry that if marijuana is legalized for medical use, there will be an increase in the number of people using it recreationally. They argue that legalization—even if it is only for therapeutic purposes—will undermine the nation's drug laws and make it more difficult to prevent illegal drug use. The Drug Free America Foundation explains: "Legalizing smoked marijuana, giving it the government's stamp of approval, sends the message to kids that drug use is not only harmless, but normal. This is precisely the opposite message we should be conveying."[61] Tandy describes similar observations during her visits to middle schools and high schools across the country, where she finds youth who have heard the arguments of medical marijuana advocates and believe marijuana must be good for you because it is used as medicine. An editorial in the *Boston Globe* argues that there is no evidence to support fears that controlled legalization will lead to increased recreational use. "Morphine, far more dangerous than marijuana, has been

> " Medical marijuana opponents. . . . argue that legalization . . . will undermine the nation's drug laws. "

prescribed by doctors for years," says the *Globe*, "with no corresponding surge in its availability on the street."[62] The Drug Policy Alliance is also critical of arguments that allowing medical marijuana will undermine national drug prevention efforts. It cites data from the California Student Survey showing that following the passage of medical marijuana legislation in California, use among ninth-graders there dropped 44 percent, and use among seventh-graders dropped 34 percent.

## A Widespread Debate

In the United States, many citizens and prominent medical professional organizations are actively involved in the debate over medical marijuana. There is substantial official support for medical legalization. In addition to a majority of the general public, the American Academy of Family Physicians, the American Nurses Association, the American Public Health Organization, and the *New England Journal of Medicine* support medical marijuana. Furthermore, no state has ever rejected a federal marijuana initiative, and twelve states have passed laws legalizing medical marijuana use. According to The National Organization for the Reform of Marijuana Lawas (NORML), in addition, twenty states have medical efficacy statutes affirming the medical value of marijuana. However, there is also much official opposition to medical marijuana. It is illegal at the federal level, and attempts to change its status as a controlled substance on FDA drug schedules have repeatedly failed. There are a number of prominent organizations that do not support the use of medical marijuana, including the American Medical Association, the British Medical Association, and the National Multiple Sclerosis Society. The issues that continue to provoke controversy include assessments of marijuana's medicinal value, the effects of smoking it, the viability of alternative drugs, and the potential social impact of medical legalization.

> " **No state has ever rejected a federal marijuana initiative.** "

# Primary Source Quotes*

# Should Medical Marijuana Be Legal?

" Marijuana . . . [has] a high potential for abuse, no currently accepted medical use in treatment in the United States, and a lack of accepted safety for use of the drug . . . under medical supervision. "

—Office of National Drug Control Policy, "Drug Facts: Marijuana," February 27, 2006. www.whitehousedrugpolicy.gov.

The Office of National Drug Control Policy was established in 1988 with the goal of eradicating illicit drug manufacture, sale, and use in the United States. It also works to eliminate drug-related crime, violence, and health consequences.

" If herbal marihuana is without any medical utility, as the US government claims, why would thousands of patients risk running afoul of the law to obtain and use it? "

—Lester Grinspoon, "History of Cannabis as a Medicine," DEA statement, August 16, 2005. www.maps.org.

Medical marijuana advocate Lester Grinspoon is an associate professor emeritus of psychiatry at Harvard Medical School. He is the author of *Marihuana Reconsidered* and *Marijuana: The Forbidden Medicine*, and maintains a Web site (www.marijuana-uses.com) dedicated to educating people about marijuana use.

" Marijuana relieves nausea, vomiting and pain, and often does so when conventional medicines fail. Marijuana helped me stay alive, as it has done for many thousands of Americans. "

—Martin Chilcutt, "U.S. Needs to Legalize Medical Marijuana," *Kalamazoo Gazette*, July 4, 2006.

Chilcutt, a resident of Kalamazoo, Michigan, has used medical marijuana to relieve nausea and other symptoms associated with cancer treatments.

* Editor's Note: While the definition of a primary source can be narrowly or broadly defined, for the purposes of Compact Research, a primary source consists of: 1) results of original research presented by an organization or researcher; 2) eyewitness accounts of events, personal experience, or work experience; 3) first-person editorials offering pundits' opinions; 4) government officials presenting political plans and/or policies; 5) representatives of organizations presenting testimony or policy.

**❝A past evaluation . . . concluded that no sound scientific studies supported medical use of marijuana for treatment in the United States, and no animal or human data supported the safety or efficacy of marijuana for general medical use. . . . FDA . . . [does] not support the use of smoked marijuana for any medical purposes.❞**

—Food and Drug Administration, "Inter-Agency Advisory Regarding Claims That Smoked Marijuana Is a Medicine," April 20, 2006.

The Food and Drug Administration is an agency of the U.S. Department of Health and Human Services and is responsible for approving and regulating the manufacture, labeling, and distribution of food and drugs in the United States.

**❝Federal Law should be changed to treat marijuana like any other legal medication, available through pharmacies upon a doctor's prescription.❞**

—Marijuana Policy Project, "State-by-State Medical Marijuana Laws: How to Remove the Threat of Arrest," June 2006.

As the largest marijuana policy reform organization in the United States, the Marijuana Policy Project works to minimize the harmful misconceptions associated with marijuana. It focuses on removing criminal penalites for marijuana use, particularly for sick people who have the approval of a doctor.

**❝Legitimizing smoked marijuana as a 'medicine' is a serious threat to the health and safety of all Americans.❞**

—Robert L. DuPont, "Marijuana and Medicine: The Need for a Science-Based Approach," testimony before the House Committee on Government Reform, Subcommittee on Criminal Justice, Drug Policy, and Human Resources, April 1, 2004.

DuPont served as the first director of the National Institute on Drug Abuse and the second director of the White House Drug Office. He is the founding president of the Anxiety Disorders Association of America and the author of numerous articles and books on drugs and addiction.

**❝Majorities in virtually every state in the country would vote, if given the chance, to legalize medical marijuana.❞**

—Ethan A. Nadelmann, "An End to Marijuana Prohibition: The Drive to Legalize Picks Up," *National Review*, July 12, 2004.

Nadelmann is founder and executive director of the Drug Policy Alliance, an organization promoting drug policy reform and alternatives to the government's war on drugs.

66 The DEA . . . ignore[s] seven statewide referenda where the public voted overwhelmingly for medical marijuana. . . . They've ignored efforts to negotiate to resolve the matter and ensure safe access for the seriously ill. Despite . . . overwhelming public support, our democratic will is still being pushed aside by the Federal Government. . . . As individuals we must challenge them. 99

—Kevin Zeese, "Why I Am Willing to Go to Jail for Medical Marijuana," July 14, 2005. http://kevinzeese.com.

Zeese is an American politician and Green/Libertarian/Populist candidate for the 2006 U.S. Senate seat from Maryland.

66 Scientific research has not demonstrated that smoked marijuana is helpful as medicine. Questions of medicine are for the FDA and medical community to answer—not special interest groups, not individuals, not public opinion. 99

—Drug Free America Foundation, "Medical 'Excuse' Marijuana," May 22, 2006. www.dfaf.org.

The Drug Free America Foundation is a drug prevention organization committed to developing policies and laws that will reduce illegal drug use, drug addiction, and drug-related injury and death. It believes that marijuana legalization will be harmful to the United States.

66 Sensible physicians . . . consider it unethical to expose individuals to the risks associated with [marijuana]. . . . There is a variety of existing, scientifically proven options available to patients in need of pain relief. Among these is the FDA-approved medicine Marinol. 99

—Andrea Barthwell, "Marijuana Is Not Medicine," *Chicago Tribune,* February 17, 2004, p. 19.

Barthwell is former deputy director of the White House Office of National Drug Control Policy and a past president of the American Society of Addiction Medicine.

**66**Marinol is an acceptable, if not ideal, substitute for whole cannabis.**99**

—Steve Kubby, "After 7 Long Years—Victory at Last!" *Kubby Chronicles*, May 19, 2006.

Kubby suffers from adrenal cancer and is a medical marijuana advocate.

**66**Marinol . . . often provides only limited relief to a select group of patients, particularly when compared to natural cannabis . . . and many experience unwanted side effects. . . . Federal and state laws should be amended to allow . . . the ability to use natural cannabis.**99**

—Paul Armentano, "Marinol Versus Natural Cannabis: Pros, Cons and Options for Patients," National Organization for the Reform of Marijuana Laws, August 11, 2005.

Armentano is a senior policy analyst for the National Organization for the Reform of Marijuana Laws, an organization working to reform marijuana laws around the world.

**66**However cultural attitudes to street or home-grown cannabis change, its availability in standardised, licensed preparations . . . will be the key to its wider medical use.**99**

—Clare Wilson, "Cannabis: Prescribing the Miracle Weed," *New Scientist*, February 5, 2005.

Wilson is a contributor to *New Scientist*, a weekly online and print science and technology news magazine.

**66**It is a mistake to rely upon laboratory creations and ignore the benefits of a naturally occurring plant that has been used for medicine since 3000 B.C.**99**

—Alan Young, "Making Canada a Leader in Medical Marijuana," *National Post*, May 3, 2006, p. A19.

Young teaches law at Osgoode Hall Law School and criminology at the University of Toronto. His work contributed to the establishment of Canada's first medical marijuana program.

# Facts and Illustrations

## Should Medical Marijuana Be Legal?

- In a November 2004 American Association of Retired Persons poll 72 percent of respondents agreed with the statement, "Adults should be allowed to legally use marijuana for medical purposes if a physician recommends it."

- On September 6, 1988, the Drug Enforcement Administration's chief administrative law judge, Francis L. Young, ruled: "Marijuana, in its natural form, is one of the safest therapeutically active substances known."

- In August 2005 the *New England Journal of Medicine* reported that an estimated 115,000 people have obtained marijuana recommendations from doctors in the United States.

- In a July 2005 telephone survey, the Congressional Research Survey found a total of 14,758 medical marijuana users in eight states with medical marijuana laws.

- Oregon's medical marijuana law—the first to be passed in the United States—was approved by 55 percent of voters.

- According to a 2005 British survey reported in the *Journal of Pain and Symptom Management,* one-third of more than five hundred HIV/AIDS patients use natural cannabis to relieve their symptoms.

# Poll on Medical Marijuana

The following poll was conducted between June 8 and June 11, 2005, by Mason-Dixon Polling & Research. Researchers conducted telephone interviews of 732 registered voters, and from this random sample, they concluded that the majority of Americans support the use of medical marijuana.

**QUESTION: Should the federal government prosecute medical marijuana patients now that it has been given the okay to do so by the U.S. Supreme Court?**

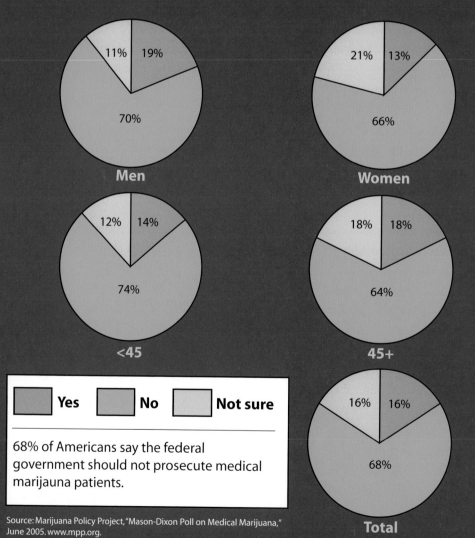

Men — 11% / 19% / 70%

Women — 21% / 13% / 66%

<45 — 12% / 14% / 74%

45+ — 18% / 18% / 64%

**Yes** **No** **Not sure**

68% of Americans say the federal government should not prosecute medical marijauna patients.

Total — 16% / 16% / 68%

Source: Marijuana Policy Project, "Mason-Dixon Poll on Medical Marijuana," June 2005. www.mpp.org.

**QUESTION: Do you think adults should be allowed to legally use marijuana for medical purposes if their doctor recommends it, or do you think that marijuana should remain illegal even for medical purposes?**

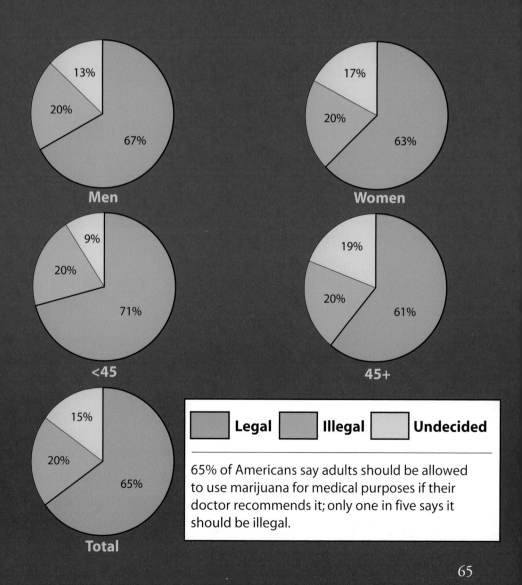

Men
- 13%
- 20%
- 67%

Women
- 17%
- 20%
- 63%

<45
- 9%
- 20%
- 71%

45+
- 19%
- 20%
- 61%

Total
- 15%
- 20%
- 65%

Legal  Illegal  Undecided

65% of Americans say adults should be allowed to use marijuana for medical purposes if their doctor recommends it; only one in five says it should be illegal.

## Medical Marijuana Laws by State

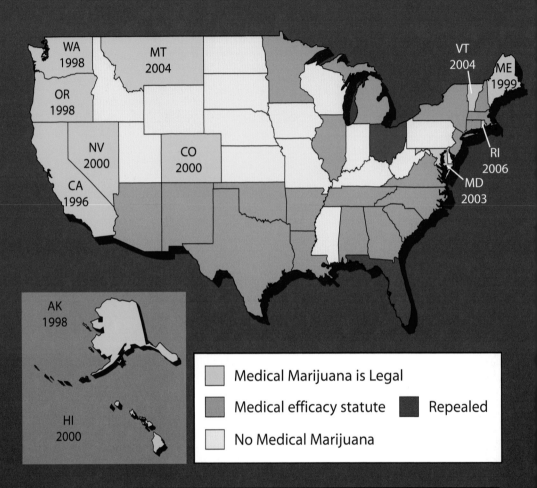

WA
1998

MT
2004

OR
1998

NV
2000

CO
2000

CA
1996

VT
2004

ME
1999

RI
2006

MD
2003

AK
1998

HI
2000

Medical Marijuana is Legal

Medical efficacy statute

Repealed

No Medical Marijuana

This map shows the status of medical marijuana laws in the United States. Twelve states have laws allowing for the use of medical marijuana, and twenty states have medical efficacy statutes affirming the medical value of marijuana. Eighteen states do not recognize any medical value of marijuana.

Source: National Organization for the Reform of Marijuana Laws, Oregon, "Medical Marijuana in the United States," 2006. www.ornorml.org.

- According to the Drug Enforcement Administration, 40 percent of medical marijuana is used for chronic pain, 22 percent for AIDS-related symptoms, and 15 percent for mood disorders.

- According to policy analyst Paul Armentano, Marinol costs a patient $200 to $800 per month, depending on dosage.

## Oregon's Medical Marijuana Program

| Patient Characteristics | |
|---|---|
| Total Number | 3,003 |
| Average Age (range) | 46 (18–87) |
| Disease/Condition* | |
| Severe Pain | 1,760 (58%) |
| Spasms | 676 (23%) |
| Nausea | 154 (5%) |
| HIV | 98 (3%) |
| Cancer | 88 (3%) |
| Cachexia | 43 (1%) |
| Seizures | 71 (2%) |
| Glaucoma | 43 (1%) |

* percentages may total more than 100% because many patients report multiple symptoms

This chart gives details on Oregon's medical marijuana program for 2002. It shows the total number of registered marijuana users in that state, and their average age. It also shows what diseases or conditions marijuana is used for by these patients.

Source: Marijuana Policy Project, "State-By-State Medical Marijuana Laws: How to Remove the Threat of Arrest." July 2004. www.mpp.org.

## Marijuana Use by Youth

| Rank | State | % | Rank | State | % |
|------|-------|------|------|-------|------|
| 1 | **Vermont** | 13.32 | 11 | **Nevada** | 9.58 |
| 2 | **Montana** | 12.07 | 12 | South Dakota | 9.57 |
| 3 | New Hampshire | 11.79 | 13 | Delaware | 9.41 |
| 4 | **Alaska** | 11.08 | 14 | **Oregon** | 9.31 |
| 5 | **Rhode Island** | 10.86 | 15 | Michigan | 9.23 |
| 6 | **Maine** | 10.56 | 16 | Connecticut | 9.22 |
| 7 | Massachusetts | 10.53 | 17 | Nebraska | 9.13 |
| 8 | New Mexico | 10.35 | 18 | **Washington** | 9.11 |
| 9 | **Hawaii** | 10.23 | 19 | Minnesota | 8.92 |
| 10 | **Colorado** | 9.82 | 20 | New York | 8.76 |

This chart ranks states by percentage of youth age twelve to seventeen reporting past-month marijuana use. Statistics are for 2002 to 2004. States with laws allowing the use of medical marijuana are in bold. Of the twenty states with the highest percentage of youth using marijuana, half are states with medical marijuana laws.

Source: Mark Eddy, "Medical Marijuana: Review and Analysis of Federal and State Policies," *Congressional Research Service*, December 29, 2005.

- The U.S. Penal Code states that a person can be imprisoned for up to one year for possession of one marijuana cigarette and imprisoned for up to five years for growing a single marijuana plant.

- According to the Marijuana Policy Project, 99 percent of all marijuana arrests are made by state and local, not federal, officials, so state medical marijuana laws can protect the majority of medical marijuana users.

# Should Marijuana Be Legalized?

For as long as there have been laws prohibiting the use and sale of marijuana, there has been debate over such laws. In the United States and elsewhere, many people argue that marijuana is undeserving of its illegal status, and should be decriminalized—meaning that criminal penalties for its use would be reduced or abolished—or legalized altogether. Author Eric Schlosser points out that in modern society many other drugs, some of them arguably more harmful than marijuana, are legal, widely available, and in common use. He cites the example of alcohol, calling it "perhaps the most dangerous drug widely consumed in the United States." "It is literally poisonous," says Schlosser, "you can die after drinking too much."[63] He claims that alcohol is linked to almost half of violent crime in the United States, and two-thirds of domestic abuse, and points out that, unlike marijuana, its commercial prodution and sale is not prohibited by the federal government.

However, opponents of such arguments maintain that regardless of the status of alcohol and other drugs, marijuana is a harmful substance that hurts both society and the individual, and should remain illegal. In the United States, Office of National Drug Control Policy (ONDCP) director John P. Walters insists, "The truth is, there are laws against marijuana because marijuana is harmful. With every year that passes, medical research discovers greater dangers from smoking it, from links to serious mental illness to the risk of cancer, and even dangers from in utero exposure [from mother to fetus]."[64] The U.S. Drug Enforcement Administration (DEA) concurs: "Illegal drugs are illegal because they are harmful."[65] Yet despite firm government opposition, marijuana advocates continue to push for legalization. Debate over the legal status of marijuana centers on whether enforcement of current marijuana laws is fair or effective, whether prohibition violates the principle of free choice, how prohibition impacts society, and what the effects of legalization might be.

## Enforcing Marijuana Laws

The United States spends billions of dollars annually to arrest and punish marijuana offenders, an amount that has steadily increased in recent years.

> **Despite firm government opposition, marijuana advocates continue to push for legalization.**

In 2005 the Sentencing Project, a Washington-based think tank, released a national analysis of marijuana offenders for the period between 1990 and 2002. According to the report, while overall arrests nationwide decreased 3 percent in that period, marijuana arrests increased 113 percent. Almost half of all drug arrests between 1990 and 2002 were for marijuana. At the same time, researchers found that while arrests have increased, the price of marijuana has decreased by 16 percent, potency has increased by 53 percent, and the level of use has remained about the same. Their conclusion: Punishing those who use marijuana does not appear to decrease marijuana use. They state, "Police spend a significant amount of time arresting marijuana users, many of whom do not merit being charged in court. This diverts efforts away from more significant criminal activity while having no appreciable impact on marijuana cost, availability, or use."[66] Similar study findings have led to the suggestion that a better policy might be to decriminalize or legalize marijuana.

Obviously, there are numerous opponents to such an approach. The DEA maintains that by strictly enforcing its drug laws, the United States has made significant progress in reducing both drug use and crime. It insists that because marijuana is illegal and obtaining and possessing it carries legal risk, its price actually remains higher than if the drug were legal. U.S. Representative Mark Souder agrees that the element of risk deters people from using marijuana. To support his point, Souder gives the example of states that allow medical marijuana. Allowing medical marijuana use makes the drug seem less risky, says Souder, increasing use by the general population. According to Sounder, statistics back up this theory. He maintains that states allowing medical marijuana have some of the highest marijuana addiction rates in the country.

> " Statistics. . . . [show] that states allowing medical marijuana have some of the highest marijuana addiction rates in the country. "

## Free Choice

Some proponents of legalization base their case on the premise that responsible adults should have the freedom to use marijuana if they choose to do so. In the opinion of the National Organization for the Reform of Marijuana Laws (NORML), marijuana prohibition is unfair because it punishes adults who use the drug responsibly. The organization stresses that children should be prevented from using marijuana, but believes that the government should not infringe on the right of adults to safely use marijuana. Says NORML, "Cannabis consumption is for adults only. . . . Children do not drive cars, enter into contracts, or marry, and they must not do drugs. As it is unrealistic to demand a lifetime abstinence from cars, contracts and marriage however, it is unrealistic to demand lifetime abstinence from all intoxicants."[67] Journalist George Lewis agrees that society should not attempt to control everything that could pose a risk to its members. That conflicts with the idea of a free society, he says: "The fact that use of a product by some people can possibly result in harm to themselves or others is no reason to forbid it in a free society."[68]

DEA administrator Karen P. Tandy contends that marijuana use is not simply a matter of personal choice and responsibility. When an individual chooses to use marijuana, he or she hurts society as a whole, she maintains. Tandy likens the issue to cigarette smoke and the fact that even nonsmokers can be harmed by secondhand smoke. "Ask . . . people about secondhand smoke from cigarettes, and they'll quickly acknowledge the harm that befalls nonsmokers," says Tandy. "We need to apply the same common-sense thinking to the even more pernicious secondhand effects of drug use."[69] While secondhand marijuana smoke is not a serious problem in society, there are other harmful secondhand effects of this drug, such as traffic accidents from marijuana-impaired driving, says Tandy. She believes marijuana must remain illegal for the protection of society.

## Effects of Current Policies

Many legalization advocates believe, however, that marijuana-related problems actually stem from the fact that the drug is illegal. They argue that the illegal status of marijuana causes crime and a black market, and insist that if marijuana were legalized, these problems could be eliminated. Journalist Jerry Stratton explains that when a substance is illegal, its production and consumption continue, but in an uncontrolled manner. This often leads to further crime. The people involved, he says, "are already breaking the law. Breaking more laws doesn't scare them."[70] Medical anthropologist Merrill Singer disagrees, arguing that it is impossible to prevent a black market in marijuana. He explains, "Being easy to grow, and because demand makes it so profitable to do so, it is all but impossible for any group, however great their resources, to maintain control over the means of marijuana production."[71] Deputy chief and executive officer of the New York City Police Department Narcotics Division Edmund Hartnett agrees, insisting that even if marijuana were legalized, drug dealers and addicts will not suddenly become productive, law-abiding members of society. "Dealers will still be involved in crime and violence," he says, "and . . . users will still need to support themselves by engaging in criminal activity."[72]

> When a substance is illegal, its production and consumption continue, but in an uncontrolled manner.

Another critique of marijuana policy is that use is occurring regardless of what the law says, and by prohibiting marijuana, the government actually has less control over how it is used. As columnist Gary Cartwright explains, "Making drugs illegal doesn't help keep them out of the hands of kids." He says, "School children can't buy hard liquor, but drugs are as available as candy on the black market."[73] Cartwright and others suggest instead that the government look to the example of alcohol. Consumption of this substance is regulated and legal for adults, with laws to prevent underage use. The same strategy could be used for marijuana, many people maintain. Says NORML policy analyst Paul Armentano, "Health risks connected with drug use . . . should not be seen as legitimate reasons for criminal prohibition, but instead as reasons for legal regulation."[74] If we legalize marijuana like we do alcohol, says Armentano, the government can better prevent youth from gaining access to it.

> " Marijuana . . . use is occurring regardless of what the law says. "

Many people say this is the wrong approach. They maintain that the best way to protect society from the dangers of marijuana it to prohibit it. Using the same example of alcohol, Walters points out that underage drinking is a widespread problem despite laws against it, and says, "Legalization will not eliminate marijuana use among young people any more than legalizing alcohol eliminated underage drinking."[75] In fact, says Walters, regular alcohol use is eight times that of marijuana. He attributes the lesser marijuana use to laws forbidding it. Walters further argues that in comparison to alcohol, marijuana is very easy to produce, so even if marijuana were legalized it would be very difficult to keep youth or anyone else from getting and using unregulated supplies. Says Walters, "The legalization scheme is . . . unworkable. A government-sanctioned program to produce, distribute, and tax an addictive intoxicant creates more problems than it solves."[76]

## Government Spending on Prohibition

Legalization advocates point to numerous potential benefits of legalizing marijuana. It could be taxed like tobacco and liquor, they suggest, boosting federal and state treasuries. In a 2005 report, professor Jeffrey A. Miron calculates that legalization would generate between $2.4 and $6.2 billion in tax revenue yearly (depending on the tax rate used), and reduce government expenditures by $7.7 billion. Legalization would also allow law enforcement resources to be used on more important issues, argue advocates. According to a 2005 report by the Sentencing Project, police currently spend $2.1 billion every year to enforce marijuana laws. If this money is not spent on marijuana enforcement, law enforcement budgets would not necessarily shrink, criminal justice expert James Austin argues: Legalization or decriminalization would allow the resources of the criminal justice system to be used more effectively. According to Austin, "Our money and resources would be better spent on far more pressing social and public safety issues."[77]

> According to a 2005 report . . . police currently spend $2.1 billion every year to enforce marijuana laws.

The DEA contends that this perspective ignores the additional costs that would be incurred if marijuana were legal. According to the administration, if marijuana were legalized, there would be increases in addiction, car accidents, illnesses, and a decline in workplace productivity that all carry high costs: "Compared to the social costs of drug abuse and addiction . . . government spending on drug control is minimal."[78] In addition, says the DEA, if marijuana were legal, crime would increase, thus actually increasing costs in the criminal justice system.

## Legalization and Levels of Use

One concern that commonly arises in any discussion of legalization or decriminalization is the effect such policies might have on marijuana use. Legalization opponents stress that it is only logical that the use of a drug increases when it is legalized. According to Tandy, that is exactly what has happened in the Netherlands following marijuana decriminalization. She also maintains that "marijuana use by Canadian teenagers is at a 25-year peak in the wake of an aggressive decriminalization movement."[79] According to Walters, increasing use is actually the goal of legalization proponents: "Drug legalization is a worldwide movement, the goal of which is to make drug consumption . . . an acceptable practice."[80]

Others disagree, finding no evidence that legalizing or decriminalizing marijuana will make a significant difference to levels of use. In a December 15, 2005, editorial in the *Bangor Daily News,* a writer argues that although there might be an initial increase in use, people will soon get over the novelty of legal marijuana, and its use will decline again. Austin agrees: "If one looks at selected studies of jurisdictions that have decriminalized the drug, the evidence is either no increase or a slight increase among those segments most likely to use the drug."[81] Founder of the Marijuana Policy Project Rob Kampia points to the example of California, which passed Proposition 215 in 1996, allowing for the use of medical marijuana there. According to Kampia, marijuana use in California by teens was rising until after the 1996 passage of the medical marijuana law, after which it started to fall dramatically. Critics of current laws add that when it comes to marijuana use, prohibition has not been successful in preventing use, so there is nothing to lose by decriminalizing or legalizing it. According to journalist William F. Buckley Jr., "Today we have illegal marijuana for whoever wants it."[82]

> **Approximately one-third of Americans believe marijuana should be legal.**

## Increasing Support for Legalization

According to a nationwide Gallup poll in November 2005, approximately one-third of Americans believe marijuana should be legal. While this number represents a minority of citizens, Gallup points out that it is an increase over past years. In 1977 only about a quarter of Americans supported the legalization of marijuana, and in 1969, just 12 percent endorsed it. Debate will likely continue into the future on the effectiveness of current marijuana policies, the constitutionality of prohibition, and theories about the impacts of both prohibition and legalization on society.

# Should Marijuana Be Legalized?

66 The use of marijuana needs to be discouraged to protect individual and community health, not encouraged by legalizing [it]. 99

—Paul M. Worrell, "Marijuana Should Remain Illegal," *Anchorage Daily News*, October 30, 2004, p. B8.

Worrell is president of the Alaska State Medical Association.

................................................................

66 Illicit substance use can be harmful to a person's health and well-being, as well as a detriment to society as a whole. It is, therefore, important to . . . build a cultural norm that views illicit drug use as unacceptable. This culture . . . works as a bulwark against the spread of drug use. 99

—Office of National Drug Control Policy, "National Drug Control Strategy," February 2006.

The Office of National Drug Control Policy was established in 1988 with the goal of eradicating illicit drug manufacture, sale, and use in the United States. It also works to eliminate drug-related crime, violence, and negative health consequences.

................................................................

66 Individuals ought to be able to make decisions [about marijuana use] themselves and pay the consequences. That's called freedom. 99

—George Lewis, "Marijuana Proposal Promotes Freedom," *Gazette (Colorado Springs)*, January 19, 2006, p. M7.

Lewis is a copy editor and writer for the *Colorado Springs Gazette*.

................................................................

* Editor's Note: While the definition of a primary source can be narrowly or broadly defined, for the purposes of Compact Research, a primary source consists of: 1) results of original research presented by an organization or researcher; 2) eyewitness accounts of events, personal experience, or work experience; 3) first-person editorials offering pundits' opinions; 4) government officials presenting political plans and/or policies; 5) representatives of organizations presenting testimony or policy.

66 Marijuana is the only drug that controls my chronic pain and motor tics. . . . It's wrong to make me live in fear of arrest for using a doctor-approved medicine that works. 99

—Warren Dolbashian, "Life of Pain, or Life of Crime?" *Call,* May 29, 2005. www.woonsocketcall.com

Dolbashian is a resident of Cranston, Rhode Island. He uses marijuana to relieve chronic pain and the symptoms of Tourette's syndrome.

66 People who smoke too much marijuana should be treated the same way as people who drink too much alcohol. They need help, not the threat of arrest, imprisonment and unemployment. 99

—Eric Schlosser, "Make Peace with Pot," *New York Times,* April 26, 2004, p. A19.

Schlosser is the author of *Fast Food Nation* and *Reefer Madness.*

66 A false characterization continues to be promoted that depicts the criminal-justice response to marijuana violations as unduly harsh, exclusively punitive, and disproportionate. . . . The truth . . . is this: Americans are not routinely being sent to prison in large numbers just for possessing small amounts of marijuana. 99

—Office of National Drug Control Policy, "Who's Really in Prison for Marijuana?" 2004. www.whitehousedrugpolicy.gov.

The Office of National Drug Control Policy was established in 1988 with the goal of eradicating illicit drug manufacture, sale, and use in the United States. It also works to eliminate drug-related crime, violence, and adverse health consequences.

66 What is empirically evident is that the growth in marijuana arrests over the 1990s has not led to a decrease in use or availability, nor an increase in cost. 99

—Ryan S. King and Marc Mauer, "The War on Marijuana: The Transformation of the War on Drugs in the 1990s," *Sentencing Project,* May 2005.

King is a research associate and Mauer is assistant director of the Sentencing Project, a nonprofit organization engaged in research and advocacy on criminal justice policy issues.

66 No student of supply-and-demand curves can doubt that marijuana would become cheaper, more readily available, and more widespread than it currently is when all legal risk is removed and demand is increased by marketing. 99

—John P. Walters, "No Surrender: The Drug War Saves Lives," *National Review*, September 27, 2004.

Walters was sworn in as the director of the White House Office of National Drug Control Policy in 2001. He coordinates all aspects of federal drug programs and spending. Since taking office, Walters has aggressively pursued the goal of reducing marijuana use by youth.

66 Our findings do not support claims that criminalization reduces cannabis use and that decriminalization increases cannabis use. . . . Dutch decriminalization does not appear to be associated with greater use of illicit drugs relative to San Francisco, nor does criminalization in San Francisco appear to be associated with less use. 99

—Craig Reinarman, Peter D.A. Cohen, and Hendrien L. Kaal, "The Limited Relevance of Drug Policy: Cannabis in Amsterdam and San Francisco," *American Journal of Public Health*, May 2004, p. 841.

Reinarman is a sociologist with the Department of Sociology at the University of California, Santa Cruz. Cohen and Kaal are researchers for the Centre for Drug Research at the University of Amsterdam in the Netherlands.

66 Marijuana legalization would reduce government expenditure by $7.7 billion annually. Marijuana legalization would also generate tax revenue of $2.4 billion annually if marijuana were taxed like all other goods and $6.2 billion annually if marijuana were taxed at rates comparable to those on alcohol and tobacco. 99

—Jeffrey A. Miron, "The Budgetary Implications of Marijuana Prohibition," *Marijuana Policy Project*, June 2005.

Miron is a visiting professor of economics at Harvard University. He is an expert in the economics of illegal drugs, and his writing has appeared in numerous publications, including the *Boston Herald* and the *Boston Globe*.

66 **If marijuana were legalized, the net effect to the taxpayer in criminal justice savings would be negligible.** 99

—James Austin, "Rethinking the Consequences of Decriminalizing Marijuana," National Organization for the Reform of Marijuana Laws, November 2, 2005.

Austin is president of the JFA Institute, a research center that conducts research on the causes of crime and the justice system's response to crime and offenders. Formerly he was director of the Institute on Crime, Justice, and Corrections at George Washington University in Washington, D.C.

66 **On a pragmatic level, decriminalization [of marijuana and other drugs] would take drug profits for organized crime and even terrorism out of the equation.** 99

—Cathy Young, "The Medical Pot Hysteria," *Boston Globe*, June 13, 2005.

Young is a contributing editor at *Reason* magazine and writes a regular column for the *Boston Globe*.

# Facts and Illustrations

## Should Marijuana Be Legalized?

- In a 2005 report, the Sentencing Project found that almost half of the yearly 1.5 million drug arrests in the United States are for marijuana.

- The Office of National Drug Control Policy reports that in 2001, only 2.3 percent of people sentenced in federal court for marijuana crimes received sentences for simple possession; the majority were convicted for trafficking.

- According to the Sentencing Project, while overall arrests between 1990 and 2002 decreased by 3 percent, marijuana arrests increased by 113 percent.

- The Office of National Drug Control Policy reports that in 2003, U.S. federal agencies seized more than 2.7 million pounds of marijuana.

- Professor of economics Jeffrey A. Miron estimates that in 2003 the federal government spent approximately $2.4 billion to enforce marijuana prohibition in the United States.

- According to professor of economics Jeffrey A. Miron, if marijuana was legalized and taxed at the same rate as other goods, yearly revenue would be $2.4 billion.

# Increasing Support for Legalizing Marijuana

Do you think the use of marijuana should be made legal, or not?

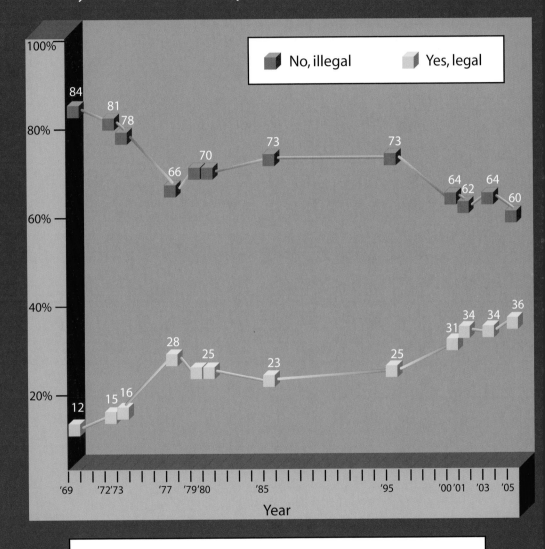

Since 1969 the Gallup poll has periodically asked Americans whether marijuana use should be made legal in the United States. This graph shows the results of these polls. It reveals that support for marijuana legalization has slowly increased since 1969.

Source: Joseph Carroll, "Who Supports Marijuana Legalization?" The Gallup Poll, November 1, 2005.

81

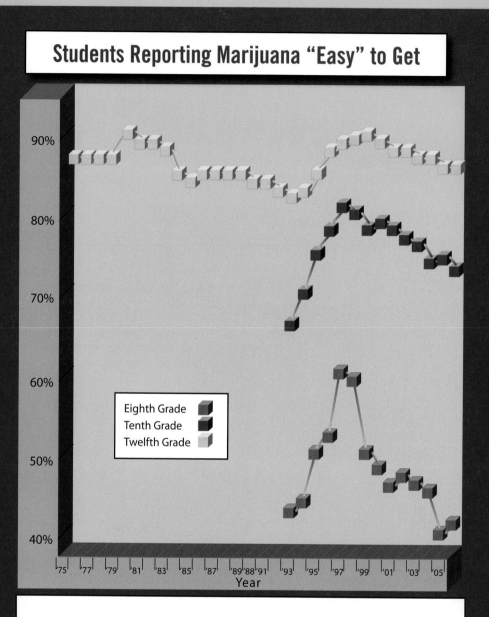

# Students Reporting Marijuana "Easy" to Get

Eighth Grade
Tenth Grade
Twelfth Grade

Year

According to this chart of marijuana availability to eighth, tenth, and twelfth graders, the percentage of students who believe marijuana is fairly easy or very easy to get has declined since the mid-1990s. Approximately 40 percent of eighth graders now report it is easy to get. However, since 1975, the number of twelfth graders who believe they can easily obtain marijuana has remained at more than 80 percent.

Source: Centers for Disease Control and Prevention, "Youth Risk Behavior Surveillance—United States, June 2006." www.cdc.gov.

- A 2003 Zogby poll reported that two out of five respondents believe the government should regulate, control, and tax marijuana as it does alcohol.

- In 2003 the Partnership for a Drug-Free America found that 49 percent of parents said they would be "extremely upset" if their child tried marijuana, down from 53 percent in 2001.

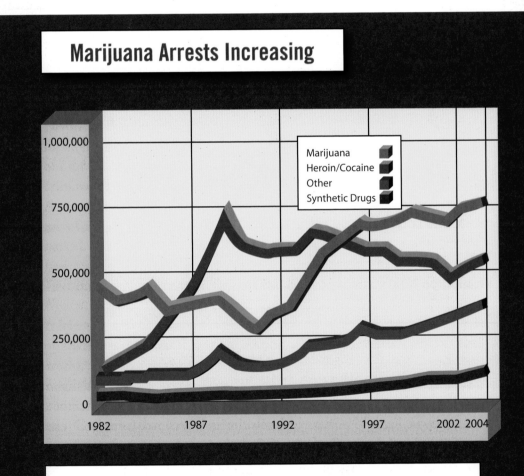

## Marijuana Arrests Increasing

This Department of Justice graph shows U.S. drug arrests between 1982 and 2004, by type of drug. It shows that since 1996, the number of arrests involving marijuana exceeded that for other types of drugs.

Source: U.S. Deparment of Justice, Office of Justice Programs, "Drug and Crime Facts," October 17, 2005. www.ojp.gov.

## Estimated Federal Costs of Marijuana Control (in millions)

| Function | Total Anti-Drug Spending | Marijuana Percentage | Marijuana Spending |
|---|---|---|---|
| Intelligence | $465.2 | 20.9% | $97.2 |
| Interdiction | $2,534.2 | 20.9% | $529.6 |
| International | $1,159.3 | 20.9% | $242.3 |
| Investigations | $2,214.5 | 20.9% | $462.8 |
| Prosecution | $112.9 | 20.9% | $23.6 |
| State and Local Assistance | $360.7 | 20.9% | $75.4 |
| **Prohibition Total Costs** | $6,846.8 | 20.9% | $1,431.0 |

The above chart shows estimates of the amount that the federal government spent on marijuana control in 2004. Enforcement of marijuana prohibition comprised an estimated 20.9 percent of all drug prohibition costs.

Source: Jeffrey A. Miron, "Federal Marijuana Policy: A Preliminary Assessment," Taxpayers for Common Sense, June 2005. www.taxpayer.net.

- In a May 2004 report in the *American Journal of Public Health*, researchers Craig Reinarman, Peter D.A. Cohen, and Hendrien L. Kaal found that while marijuana is lawfully available in Amsterdam and illegal in San Francisco, there were no differences between the two cities in the age of first marijuana use.

- According to the Canadian Addiction Survey, the number of Canadians using marijuana increased from 7.4 percent in 1994 to 14 percent in 2004.

# Key People and Advocacy Groups

**Andrea Barthwell:** Former deputy director at the White House Office of National Drug Control Policy, Andrea Barthwell is an outspoken critic of medical marijuana. She is opposed to the legalization of marijuana and in favor of random student drug testing.

**Drug Free America Foundation:** The Drug Free America Foundation is a drug prevention and policy organization committed to developing policies and laws that will reduce illegal drug use, drug addiction, and drug-related injury and death. It believes that drug legalization will be harmful to the United States.

**Mitch Earleywine:** Medical marijuana advocate Mitch Earleywine is an associate professor of psychology at the State University of New York at Albany, where he teaches drugs and human behavior, substance abuse treatment, and clinical research methods. He has written more than fifty publications on drug use and abuse and is the author of the book *Understanding Marijuana*.

**Lester Grinspoon:** Medical marijuana advocate Lester Grinspoon is an associate professor emeritus of psychiatry at Harvard Medical School. He is the author of *Marihuana Reconsidered* and *Marijuana: The Forbidden Medicine*, and maintains a Web site (www.marijuana-uses.com) dedicated to educating people about marijuana use.

**Rob Kampia:** Kampia is an activist for marijuana policy reform. In 1995 he founded the Marijuana Policy Project, an organization that works to remove criminal penalties for marijuana use.

**Marijuana Policy Project (MPP):** The largest marijuana policy reform organization in the United States, MPP works to minimize the harmful associations of marijuana. It focuses on removing criminal penalites for marijuana use, particularly for sick people who have the approval of a doctor.

**Ethan Nadelmann:** Nadelmann is an outstanding proponent of drug policy reform—including marijuana policy—both in the United States and abroad. He is the founder and executive director of the Drug Policy Alliance, an organization promoting drug reform policy and alternatives to the government's war on drugs.

**National Institute on Drug Abuse (NIDA):** NIDA is a branch of the U.S. Department of Health and Human Services, and works to prevent drug abuse and addiction in the United States. The organization supports research studies on abuse and addiction, and works to educate the public about the results of this research.

**National Organization for the Reform of Marijuana Laws (NORML):** This nonprofit organization aims to legalize the responsible use of marijuana by adults. It believes criminal penalties for marijuana use should be removed and that there should be a legally controlled market for marijuana. NORML has chapters in numerous U.S. states and in other countries.

**Keith Stroup:** Attorney Keith Stoup founded the National Organization for the Reform of Marijuana Laws (NORML) in 1970 and served as both national director and executive director. He currently serves as legal counsel for NORML, and gives college lectures on marijuana policy.

**Karen P. Tandy:** Tandy is administrator of the federal Drug Enforcement Administration. She has pledged to help carry out the Bush administration's war on drugs and to pursue and prosecute medical marijuana users and providers.

**John P. Walters:** Walters was sworn in as the director of the White House Office of National Drug Control Policy in 2001. He coordinates all aspects of federal drug programs and spending. Since taking office, Walters has aggressively pursued the goal of reducing marijuana use by youth.

**White House Office of National Drug Control Policy (ONDCP):** The ONDCP was established in 1988. Its goal is to eradicate illicit drug manufacture, sale, and use in the United States. It also works to eliminate drug-related crime, violence, and negative health consequences.

# Chronology

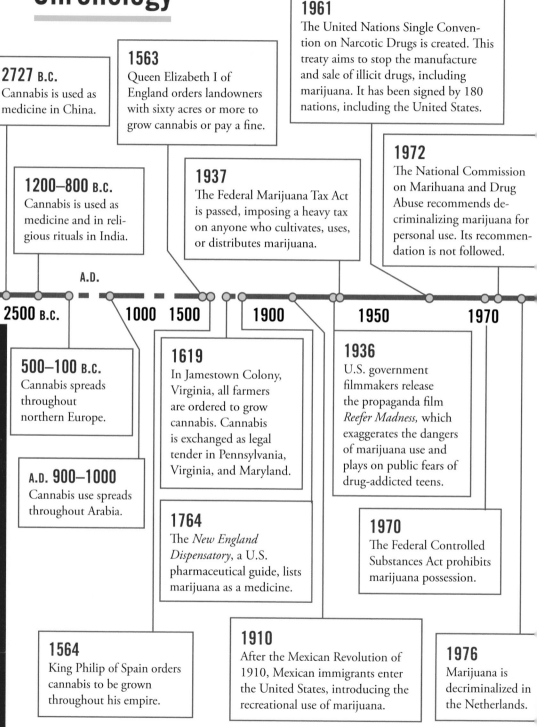

**2727 B.C.**
Cannabis is used as medicine in China.

**1563**
Queen Elizabeth I of England orders landowners with sixty acres or more to grow cannabis or pay a fine.

**1961**
The United Nations Single Convention on Narcotic Drugs is created. This treaty aims to stop the manufacture and sale of illicit drugs, including marijuana. It has been signed by 180 nations, including the United States.

**1972**
The National Commission on Marihuana and Drug Abuse recommends decriminalizing marijuana for personal use. Its recommendation is not followed.

**1200–800 B.C.**
Cannabis is used as medicine and in religious rituals in India.

**1937**
The Federal Marijuana Tax Act is passed, imposing a heavy tax on anyone who cultivates, uses, or distributes marijuana.

A.D.

2500 B.C.  1000  1500  1900  1950  1970

**500–100 B.C.**
Cannabis spreads throughout northern Europe.

**1619**
In Jamestown Colony, Virginia, all farmers are ordered to grow cannabis. Cannabis is exchanged as legal tender in Pennsylvania, Virginia, and Maryland.

**1936**
U.S. government filmmakers release the propaganda film *Reefer Madness,* which exaggerates the dangers of marijuana use and plays on public fears of drug-addicted teens.

**A.D. 900–1000**
Cannabis use spreads throughout Arabia.

**1764**
The *New England Dispensatory,* a U.S. pharmaceutical guide, lists marijuana as a medicine.

**1970**
The Federal Controlled Substances Act prohibits marijuana possession.

**1564**
King Philip of Spain orders cannabis to be grown throughout his empire.

**1910**
After the Mexican Revolution of 1910, Mexican immigrants enter the United States, introducing the recreational use of marijuana.

**1976**
Marijuana is decriminalized in the Netherlands.

**1978**
The Investigational New Drug (IND) Compassionate Access Program is established by the U.S. Food and Drug Administration (FDA). It allows patients with serious medical conditions that can only be relieved with marijuana to apply for and receive medical marijuana from the federal government.

**1998**
Oregon, Alaska, and Washington pass laws allowing the use of medical marijuana by patients with a debilitating medical condition; District of Columbia voters approve a medical marijuana initiative that is blocked by Congress.

**2003**
Maryland passes a law protecting medical marijuana users from the threat of jail.

**2004**
Great Britain changes its marijuana laws, with the result that marijuana possession is illegal, but not an arrestable offense; Montana passes a law allowing the use of medical marijuana.

**1985**
Marinol, a synthetic form of THC (delta-9-tetrahydrocannabinol), is the only cannabis-based drug to be approved by the FDA for use in the United States.

**2000**
Hawaii, Colorado, and Nevada pass laws allowing the use of medical marijuana.

**1980**     **1990**     **2000**     **2005**

**1992**
The IND Compassionate Access Program is cancelled; President Bill Clinton admits to having smoked marijuana in his youth, but claims he never inhaled.

**2002**
In *Conant v. Walters* the Ninth U.S. Court of Appeals upholds a lower court ruling that the federal government cannot punish physicians for discussing or recommending medical marijuana.

**1996**
California's Proposition 215 removes criminal penalties for medical marijuana use, possession, or cultivation by patients who have the oral or written recommendation of a physician; Arizona passes a law permitting medical marijuana prescriptions.

**2001**
In *U.S. v. Oakland Buyers' Cooperative* the Supreme Court rules that distributors of medical marijuana cannot use a defense of medical necessity against federal marijuana distribution charges; Canada becomes the first national government in the world to approve the use of medical marijuana.

**1999**
Maine passes a ballot measure allowing the use of medical marijuana; the federal government commissions the National Institute of Medicine (IOM) to review the scientific evidence on the possible benefits and risks of marijuana. The IOM report gives a qualified endorsement to medical marijuana, and recommends further research.

**2006**
The FDA issues a statement denying that marijuana has any medical benefits at all.

# Related Organizations

### Americans for Safe Access (ASA)
1322 Webster St., Suite 208
Oakland, CA 94612
Phone: (888) 929-4367
e-mail: info@safeaccessnow.org
Web site: www.safeaccessnow.org

Americans for Safe Access works to protect the rights of patients and doctors to use marijuana for medical purposes. ASA's mission is to ensure safe, legal access to marijuana for all who are helped by it. The organization provides legal training for lawyers and patients, medical information for doctors and patients, media support for court cases, and activist training to organizers.

### Common Sense for Drug Policy (CSDP)
1377-C Spencer Ave.
Lancaster, PA 17603
Phone: (717) 299-0600
Fax: (717) 393-4953
e-mail: info@csdp.org
Web site: www.csdp.org

CSDP is a nonprofit organization dedicated to reforming drug policy. The organization disseminates factual information and comments on existing laws, policies, and practices. CSDP advocates the regulation and control of marijuana in a manner similar to alcohol and subject to local, rather than federal, decisions.

### Drug Enforcement Administration (DEA)
2401 Jefferson Davis Hwy., Suite 300
Alexandria, VA 22301
Phone: (800) 882-9539
Web site: www.dea.gov

The mission of the Drug Enforcement Administration is to enforce the controlled substances laws and regulations of the United States. It coordinates the activities of federal, state, and local agencies, and works with foreign governments to reduce the availability of illicit drugs in the United States.

## Drug Free America Foundation

2600 9th St. N, Suite 200
St. Petersburg, FL 33704
Phone: (727) 828-0211
Fax: (727) 828-0212
Web site: www.dfaf.org

Drug Free America Foundation is a drug prevention and policy organization committed to developing, promoting, and sustaining global strategies, policies, and laws that will reduce illegal drug use, drug addiction, and drug-related injury and death. The organization believes that the legalization of marijuana would be harmful to society.

## Drug Policy Alliance

925 15th St. NW, 2nd Floor
Washington, DC 20005
Phone: (202) 216-0035
Fax: (202) 216-0803
e-mail: dc@drugpolicy.org
Web site: www.drugpolicy.org

The Drug Policy Alliance believes in the sovereignty of individuals over their minds and bodies. Its position is that people should be punished for crimes committed against others, but not for using marijuana or other drugs as a personal choice. It promotes alternatives to the war on drugs in the United States and works to reduce the harms of drug misuse.

## Drug Reform Coordination Network

1623 Connecticut Ave. NW, 3rd Floor
Washington, DC 20009
Phone: (202) 293-8340
Fax: (202) 293-8344
e-mail: drcnet@drcnet.org
Web site: http://stopthedrugwar.org

The Drug Reform Coordination Network is an organization of educators, students, lawyers, health care professionals, academics, and others working to reform current drug policies. The organization believes that the federal government should reschedule marijuana to permit medical use.

## Marijuana Policy Project (MPP)
PO Box 77492, Capitol Hill
Washington, DC 20013
e-mail: info@mpp.org
Web site: www.mpp.org

The Marijuana Policy Project is the largest marijuana policy reform organization in the United States. MPP works to minimize the harm associated with marijuana—both the consumption of marijuana and the laws that are intended to prohibit such use. The organization believes that the greatest harm associated with marijuana is prison, and focuses on removing criminal penalties for marijuana use. It also works to make marijuana medically available to seriously ill people who have the approval of their doctors.

## Multidisciplinary Association for Psychedelic Studies (MAPS)
2105 Robinson Ave.
Sarasota, FL 34232
Phone: (941) 924-6277
Fax: (941) 924-6265
e-mail: askmaps.org
Web site: www.maps.org

MAPS is a research and educational organization that assists scientists in conducting research on the spiritual and healing properties of marijuana and other drugs. The organization believes that marijuana has the potential to help millions of people in alleviating the symptoms of such illnesses as cancer and AIDS.

## National Institute on Drug Abuse (NIDA)
6001 Executive Blvd., Room 5213
Bethesda, MD 20892
Phone: (301) 443-1124
e-mail: information@nida.nih.gov
Web site: www.nida.nih.gov

The National Institute on Drug Abuse is one of the National Institutes of Health, a component of the U.S. Department of Health and Human Services. It supports scientific research on drug abuse and addiction. NIDA also works to disseminate the results of this research to policy makers, drug abuse practitioners, other health care practitioners, and the general public.

## National Organization for the Reform of Marijuana Laws (NORML)

1600 K St. NW, Suite 501
Washington, DC 20006
Phone: (202) 483-5500
Fax: (202) 483-0057
e-mail: norml@norml.org
Web site: www.norml.org

NORML is a public-interest advocacy group that opposes marijuana prohibition. The organization supports the right of adults to use marijuana responsibly for both personal and medical purposes. It believes that all penalties should be eliminated for responsible use. Further, NORML believes that a legally regulated market should be established where consumers can buy marijuana in a safe and secure environment.

## Office of National Drug Control Policy (ONDCP)

PO Box 6000
Rockville, MD 20849-6000
Phone: (800) 666–3332
Fax: (301) 519–5212
Web site: www.whitehousedrugpolicy.gov

The White House Office of National Drug Control Policy was established by the Anti-Drug Abuse Act of 1988. Its purpose is to establish policies, priorities, and objectives for the nation's drug control program. The goals of the program are to reduce illicit drug use, manufacturing, and trafficking; drug-related crime and violence; and drug-related health consequences.

# For Further Research

## Books

Martin Booth, *Cannabis: A History.* New York: St. Martin's, 2004.

Nick Brownlee, *The Complete Illustrated Guide to Cannabis.* London: Sanctuary, 2003.

Robert Deitch, *Hemp—American History Revisited: The Plant with a Divided History.* New York: Algora, 2003.

Joan Esherick, *Dying for Acceptance: A Teen's Guide to Drug- and Alcohol-Related Health Issues.* Philadelphia: Mason Crest, 2005.

Rudolph J. Gerber, *Legalizing Marijuana: Drug Reform Policy and Prohibition Politics.* Westport, CT: Praeger, 2004.

Ted Gottfried, *The Facts About Marijuana.* New York: Benchmark, 2005.

Geoffrey Guy, Brian A. Whittle, and Philip J. Robson, eds., *The Medicinal Use of Cannabis and Cannabinoids.* Chicago: Pharmaceutical, 2004.

Laura E. Huggins, ed., *Drug War Deadlock: The Policy Battle Continues.* Stanford, CA: Hoover Institution, 2005.

Curtis Marez, *Drug Wars: The Political Economy of Narcotics.* Minneapolis: University of Minnesota Press, 2004.

Merrill Singer, *Something Dangerous: Emergent and Changing Illicit Drug Use and Community Health.* Long Grove, IL: Waveland, 2006.

Michael K. Steinberg, Joseph J. Hobbs, and Kent Mathewson, eds., *Dangerous Harvest: Drug Plants and the Transformation of Indigenous Landscapes.* Oxford, UK: Oxford University Press, 2004.

## Periodicals

Steve Boggan, "If Cannabis Is Safe, Why Am I a Psychotic?" *Times* (London), January 7, 2004.

William F. Buckley Jr., "Free Weeds," *National Review,* June 29, 2004.

Joseph A. Califano Jr., "Cutting Marijuana Use Calls for More than Tough Policing," *Washington Post*, May 17, 2005.

Ross Clark, "Reefer Madness: Cannabis Is Not Harmless, Says Ross Clark, and Libertarians Are Wrong to Call for Its Legalisation," *Spectator,* January 28, 2006.

Sherwood O. Cole, "An Update on the Effects of Marijuana & Its Potential Medical Use: Forensic Focus," *Forensic Examiner*, Fall 2005.

Marcus Conant, "Guest Editorial: Medical Marijuana," *Family Practice News*, July 1, 2005.

Margaret Cook, "Cannabis: A Bad Trip for the Young," *New Statesman*, January 31, 2005.

*Economist*, "Reefer Madness," April 27, 2006.

Dan Eggen, "Marijuana Becomes Focus of Drug War," *Washington Post*, May 4, 2005.

Ishani Ganguli, "Growing Pot for Science," *Scientist,* February 2006.

Gary Greenberg, "Respectable Reefer," *Mother Jones*, November/December 2005.

*Harvard Health Letter*, "Reefer Rx: Marijuana as Medicine," September 2004.

Marni Jackson, "Pass the Weed, Dad," *Macleans*, November 1, 2005.

Graham Lawton, "Too Much, Too Young: Are Teenage Users Jeopardising Their Mental Health?" *New Scientist*, March 26, 2005.

Nikos A. Leverenz, "Testing the Wrong Policy on Students," *Brainwash*, September 19, 2004.

George Lewis, "Marijuana Proposal Promotes Freedom," *Gazette*, January 19, 2006.

Ethan A. Nadelmann, "An End to Marijuana Prohibition: The Drive to Legalize Picks Up," *National Review*, July 12, 2004.

———, "The Future of an Illusion: On the Drug War, Believe Your Own Eyes," *National Review*, September 27, 2004.

*National Review*, "A Case for Mercy," July 4, 2005.

Roger A. Nicoll and Bradley N. Alger, "The Brain's Own Marijuana," *Scientific American*, November 22, 2004.

Evelyn Nieves, "'I Really Consider Cannabis My Miracle': Patients Fighting to Keep Drug of Last Resort," *Washington Post*, January 1, 2005.

Debra J. Saunders, "Smoke Gets in Your Politics," *San Francisco Chronicle,* December 6, 2005.

Eric Schlosser, "Make Peace with Pot," *New York Times*, April 26, 2004.

David Sharp, "Highs and Lows of Cannabis," *Lancet*, January 31, 2004.

John P. Walters, "No Surrender: The Drug War Saves Lives," *National Review*, September 27, 2004.

Clare Wilson, "Cannabis: Prescribing the Miracle Weed," *New Scientist*, February 5, 2005.

## Internet Sources

James Austin, "Rethinking the Consequences of Decriminalizing Marijuana," National Organization for the Reform of Marijuana Laws, November 2, 2005. www.norml.org/index.cfm?Group_ID=6695.

Drug Free America Foundation, "Medical 'Excuse' Marijuana," May 22, 2006. www.dfaf.org/marijuana/excuse.php.

Ryan S. King and Marc Mauer, "The War on Marijuana: The Transformation of the War on Drugs," Sentencing Project, May 2005. www.sentencingproject.org/pdfs/waronmarijuana.pdf.

Marijuana Policy Project, "Medical Marijuana Briefing Paper: The Need to Change State and Federal Law," February 2006. www.mpp.org/site/c.glKZLeMQIsG/b.1736185/k.96AB/Medical_Marijuana_Briefing_Paper__2006.htm.

National Institute on Drug Abuse, "InfoFacts: Marijuana," April 2006. www.drugabuse.gov/infofacts/marijuana.html.

Office of National Drug Control Policy, "Drug Facts: Marijuana," February 27, 2006. www.whitehousedrugpolicy.gov/drugfact/marijuana/index.html.

# Source Notes

## Overview

1. Merrill Singer, *Something Dangerous: Emergent and Changing Illicit Drug Use and Community Health.* Long Grove, IL: Waveland., 2006, p. 49.
2. Quoted in James A. Inciardi, *The War on Drugs III: The Continuing Saga of the Mysteries and Miseries of Intoxication, Addiction, Crime, and Public Policy.* Boston: Allyn and Bacon, 2002, p. 34.
3. Emancipated, "A Way of Life," *Dr. Lester Grinspoon's Marijuana Uses,* 2006. www.marijuana-uses.com.
4. Angel McLary Raich, "Declaration of Angel McClary Raich," United States District Court for the Northern District of California C 02 4872 EMC, October 25, 2002. www.angeljustice. org.
5. Andrea Barthwell, "A Haze of Misinformation Clouds Issue of Medical Marijuana," *Los Angeles Times,* p. B13.
6. Kate Scannell, "Mr. Attorney General, Listen to the Doctors and Patients. John Ashcroft, Meet a Cancer Victim," *Americans for Safe Access,* February 20, 2003. www.safeaccessnow.org.
7. Robert L. DuPont, "Marijuana and Medicine: The Need for a Science-Based Approach," testimony before the House Committee on Government Reform, Subcommittee on Criminal Justice, Drug Policy, and Human Resources, April 1, 2004. www.ibhinc.org.
8. U.S. Food and Drug Administration, "Inter-Agency Advisory Regarding Claims That Smoked Marijuana Is a Medicine," April 20, 2006. www.fda.gov.
9. Marijuana Policy Project, "Medical Marijuana Briefing Paper: The Need to Change State and Federal Law," February 2006. www.mpp.org.
10. Robert J. Meyer, testimony before the House Committee on Government Reform, Subcommittee on Criminal Justice, Drug Policy, and Human Resources, April 1, 2004. www.fda.gov.
11. Ethan A. Nadelmann, "An End to Marijuana Prohibition: The Drive to Legalize Picks Up," *National Review,* July 12, 2004.
12. Eric Schlosser, "Make Peace with Pot," *New York Times,* April 26, 2004, p. A19.
13. Office of National Drug Control Policy, "Who's Really in Prison for Marijuana?" 2004. www.whitehousedrug policy.gov.
14. Ethan A. Nadelmann, "The Future of an Illusion: On the Drug War, Believe Your Own Eyes," *National Review,* September 27, 2004.
15. Nora D. Volkow, "Marijuana and Medicine: The Need for a Science-Based Approach," testimony before the House Committee on Government Reform, Subcommittee on Criminal Justice, Drug Policy, and Human Resources, April 1, 2004. www.drugabuse.gov.
16. Robert Deitch, *Hemp—American History Revisited: The Plant with a Divided History.* New York: Algora, 2003, pp. 226–27.

## Is Marijuana Harmful to Health?

17. Nick Brownlee, *The Complete Illustrated Guide to Cannabis.* London: Sanctuary, 2003, p. 122.
18. Sherwood O. Cole, "An Update on the Effects of Marijuana & Its Potential Medical Use: Forensic Focus," *Forensic Examiner,* Fall 2005.
19. National Institute on Drug Abuse, "InfoFacts: Marijuana," April 2006. www.nida.nih.gov.

20. David Salyer, "Medical Marijuana," *Survival News,* November/December 2005, p. 15.
21. Cole, "An Update on the Effects of Marijuana."
22. John P. Walters, "No Surrender: The Drug War Saves Lives," *National Review,* September 27, 2004.
23. European Monitoring Centre for Drugs and Drug Addiction, "An Overview of Cannabis Potency in Europe," 2004. www.emcdda.europa.eu.
24. Nadelmann, "An End to Marijuana Prohibition."
25. Karen P. Tandy, "Marijuana: The Myths Are Killing Us," *Police Chief,* March 2005. http://policechiefmagazine.org.
26. Douglas Husak, *Legalize This! The Case of Decriminalizing Drugs.* New York: Verso, 2002, p. 100.

## How Does Marijuana Use Affect Society?

27. Office of National Drug Control Policy, "What Americans Need to Know About Marijuana: Important Facts About Our Nation's Most Misunderstood Illegal Drug," October 2003. www.whitehousedrugpolicy.gov.
28. Alan Young, "And Marijuana for All," *Now Magazine Online Edition,* April 7–13, 2005. www.nowtoronto.com.
29. Office of National Drug Control Policy, "What Americans Need to Know."
30. Office of National Drug Control Policy, "What Americans Need to Know."
31. Drug Enforcement Administration, "Speaking Out Against Drug Legalization," May 2003. www.dea.gov.
32. Sheryl Jackson-Sczbecki, "Marijuana: Through the Haze," *rense.com,* February 12, 2006. www.rense.com.
33. Singer, *Something Dangerous,* p. 204.
34. National Organization for the Reform of Marijuana Laws, New Zealand, "NORML's Submission to the National Drug Policy Consultation," June 9, 2006. www.norml.org.
35. National Center on Addiction and Substance Abuse at Columbia University, "Non-Medical Marijuana II: Rite of Passage or Russian Roulette?" April 2004. www.casacolumbia.org.
36. Mitch Earleywine, "HB 96: Crimes Involving Marijuana and Other Drugs," testimony before the House Judiciary Committee, April 8, 2005. www.law.state.ak.us.
37. Earleywine, "HB 96: Crimes Involving Marijuana and Other Drugs."
38. Jackson-Sczbecki, "Marijuana Through the Haze."
39. National Institute on Drug Abuse, "InfoFacts: Marijuana."
40. National Institute on Drug Abuse, "InfoFacts: Marijuana."
41. El Sohly, "HB 96: Crimes Involving Marijuana and other Drugs," testimony before the House Judiciary Committee, April 8, 2005. www.law.state.ak.us.
42. Tasha H. Bangor, editorial, *Bangor Daily News,* December 15, 2005, p. C1.
43. Emancipated, "A Way of Life."
44. Inciardi, *The War on Drugs III,* p. 283.
45. Deitch, *Hemp—American History Revisited,* p. 227.

## Should Medical Marijuana Be Legal?

46. Marijuana Policy Project, "Medical Marijuana Briefing Paper."
47. John A. Benson Jr., "Marijuana and Medicine: Assessing the Science Base: Opening Statements by Principal Investigators," *Institute of Medicine,* March 17, 1999. www4.nationalacademies.org.
48. Tandy, "Marijuana: The Myths Are Killing Us."
49. Mark Eddy, "Medical Marijuana: Review and Analysis of Federal and State Policies," *Congressional Research Service,* December 29, 2005. www.safeaccessnow.org.

50. Drug Free America Foundation, "Medical Excuse Marijuana," May 22, 2005. www.dfaf.org.
51. Robert L. DuPont, "Marijuana and Medicine."
52. Joycelyn Elders, "Myths About Medical Marijuana," *The Providence Journal,* March 26, 2004.
53. Kate Scannell, "Mr. Attorney General, Listen to the Doctors and Patients."
54. Drug Free America Foundation, "Medical 'Fraud' Marijuana."
55. Ethan Nadelmann, interview with Gwen Ifill, "Medical Marijuana Decision," *Public Broadcasting Service Online NewsHour,* June 6, 2005. www.pbs.org.
56. Drug Free America Foundation, "Medical 'Fraud' Marijuana."
57. U.S. Drug Enforcement Administration, "Exposing the Myth of Medical Marijuana: Marijuana: The Facts," www.usdoj.gov.
58. Cole, "An Update on the Effects of Marijuana."
59. *National Review*, "A Case for Mercy," July 4, 2005, p. 12.
60. Alan Young, "Making Canada a World Leader in Medical Marijuana," *National Post*, May 3, 2006, p. A19.
61. Drug Free America Foundation, "Medical 'Fraud' Marijuana."
62. *Boston Globe*, "Marijuana Paranoia," November 30, 2004. www.boston.com.

**Should Marijuana Be Legalized?**
63. Schlosser, "Make Peace with Pot," p. A19.
64. Walters, "No Surrender: The Drug War Saves Lives."
65. Drug Enforcement Administration, "Speaking Out Against Drug Legalization."
66. Ryan S. King and Marc Mauer, "The War on Marijuana: The Transformation of the War on Drugs in the 1990s," *Sentencing Project*, May 2005.
www.sentencingproject.org.
67. National Organization for the Reform of Marijuana Laws, New Zealand, "NORML's Submission."
68. George Lewis, "Marijuana Proposal Promotes Freedom," *Gazette*, January 19, 2006, p. M7.
69. Tandy, "Marijuana: The Myths Are Killing Us."
70. Jerry Stratton, "F— Everything Except Marijuana," *Negative Space*, October 1, 2005. www.hoboes.com.
71. Singer, *Something Dangerous*, p. 139.
72. Edmund Hartnett, "Drug Legalization: Why It Wouldn't Work in the United States," *Police Chief,* March 2005. www.policechiefmagazine.com.
73. Gary Cartwright, "Weed All About It; Yes, I Think We Should Legalize Marijuana—and Maybe All Drugs. But the Big News Is That Some Prominent Conservative Republicans Agree with Me," *Texas Monthly*, July 2005.
74. Paul Armentano, "Cannabis, Mental Health and Context: The Case for Regulation," *National Organization for the Reform of Marijuana Laws*, January 27, 2006. www.norml.org.
75. Walters, "No Surrender."
76. Walters, "No Surrender."
77. James Austin, "Rethinking the Consequences of Decriminalizing Marijuana," *National Organization for the Reform of Marijuana Laws*, November 2, 2005. www.norml.org.
78. Drug Enforcement Administration, "Speaking Out Against Drug Legalization."
79. Tandy, "Marijuana: The Myths Are Killing Us."
80. Walters, "No Surrender."
81. Austin, "Rethinking the Consequences of Decriminalizing Marijuana."
82. William F. Buckley Jr., "Free Weeds," *National Review Online*, June 29, 2004. http://article.nationalreview.com.

# List of Illustrations

List of Illustrations

# Index

# About the Author

Andrea C. Nakaya, a native of New Zealand, holds a BA in English and an MA in Communication from San Diego State University. She currently lives in Encinitas, California, with her husband Jamie and their daughter Natalie. In her free time she enjoys traveling, reading, gardening, and snowboarding.